Unity Artificial Intelligence Programming

Fifth Edition

Add powerful, believable, and fun AI entities in your
game with the power of Unity

Dr. Davide Aversa

BIRMINGHAM—MUMBAI

Unity Artificial Intelligence Programming
Fifth Edition

Group Product Manager: Rohit Rajkumar
Publishing Product Manager: Ashitosh Gupta
Senior Editor: Hayden Edwards
Content Development Editor: Abhishek Jadhav
Technical Editor: Saurabh Kadave
Copy Editor: Safis Editing
Project Coordinator: Rashika Ba
Proofreader: Safis Editing
Indexer: Manju Arasan
Production Designer: Sinhayna Bais
Marketing Coordinator: Elizabeth Varghese and Teny Thomas

First published: July 2013
Second edition: September 2015
Third edition: January 2018
Fourth edition: November 2018
Fifth edition: March 2022

Production reference: 1280222

Published by Packt Publishing Ltd.
Livery Place
35 Livery Street
Birmingham
B3 2PB, UK.

ISBN 978-1-80323-853-1

www.packt.com

To my parents, Ferruccio and Sara, for their role in making me what I am today. And to my life partner, Gioia, for shaping with me what I will be tomorrow.

– Davide Aversa

Contributors

About the author

Dr. Davide Aversa holds a PhD in **Artificial Intelligence (AI)** and an MSc in AI and robotics from the University of Rome La Sapienza in Italy. He has a strong interest in AI for the development of interactive virtual agents and procedural content generation. He has served as a program committee member for video game-related conferences such as the IEEE conference on computational intelligence and games, and he also regularly participates in game-jam contests. He also writes a blog on game design and game development.

About the reviewers

Giacomo Salvadori is a game developer, lecturer, and researcher who has worked in many different environments, including private game companies, NGOs, academies, and universities. He is led by his enthusiasm and passion for games.

Giacomo's fields of expertise are game design and programming. The areas of his studies are AI and combat design. Outside work, Giacomo loves to spend time in nature and dreams of traveling the world on a boat.

Kazimieras Mikelis is a self-taught video game software engineer specializing in AI programming and technical systems design. Their first-hand expertise in game AI comes from working in many diverse companies in the industry, from close-knit start-ups to big studios building AAA games, on work ranging from small projects to cross-platform game releases.

Ardent about exploring what games can offer as a medium, Kazimieras Mikelis authors a blog on game development and enjoys unique idea-driven games in his free time.

Amir Reza Asadi is a software engineer and HCI researcher interested in using video games to solve real-world problems. He is chair of the Metaverse ACM SIGCHI chapter. He has also served as a reviewer for several high-profile conferences, including ACM CHI and IEEE VR.

As an entrepreneur and owner of Humind Labs, he has launched various start-up projects, including BeyondBoard AR. He aims to design novel experiences for emerging technologies such as XR. On this adventure, he has written multiple papers and acquired knowledge of various technologies, including Unity.

He is currently leading the design and development of Fashionator, a digital fashion design platform. In his spare time, he studies the intersection of digital twins and AI in the Metaverse.

Table of Contents

3

Randomness and Probability

4

Implementing Sensors

Part 2: Movement and Navigation

5
Flocking

6
Path Following and Steering Behaviors

7
A* Pathfinding

11

Machine Learning in Unity

12

Putting It All Together

Index

Other Books You May Enjoy

Preface

Developing **Artificial Intelligence** (**AI**) for game characters in Unity has never been easier. Unity provides game and app developers with a variety of tools to implement AI, from basic techniques to cutting-edge machine learning-powered agents. Leveraging these tools via Unity's API or built-in features allows limitless possibilities when it comes to creating game worlds and characters.

This updated fifth edition of *Unity Artificial Intelligence Programming* starts by breaking down AI into simple concepts. Using a variety of examples, the book then takes those concepts and walks you through actual implementations designed to highlight key concepts and features related to game AI in Unity. As you progress, you'll learn how to implement a **Finite State Machine** (**FSM**) to determine how your AI behaves, apply probability and randomness to make games less predictable, and implement a basic sensory system. Later, you'll understand how to set up a game map with a navigation mesh, incorporate movement through techniques such as A* pathfinding, and provide characters with decision-making abilities using behavior trees.

By the end of this Unity book, you'll have the skills you need to bring together all the concepts and practical lessons you've learned to build an impressive vehicle battle game.

Who this book is for

This Unity AI book is for Unity developers with a basic understanding of C# and the Unity Editor who want to expand their knowledge of AI Unity game development.

What this book covers

Chapter 1, Introduction to AI, talks about what AI is and how it is used in games. We also discuss the various techniques used to implement AI in games.

Chapter 2, Finite State Machines, discusses a way of simplifying how we manage the decisions that AI needs to make. We use FSMs to determine how AI behaves in a particular state and how it transitions to other states.

Chapter 3, Randomness and Probability, discusses the basics behind probability, and how to change the probability of a particular outcome. Then we look at how to add randomness to our game to make the AI less predictable.

Chapter 4, Implementing Sensors, looks at making our characters aware of the world around them. With the ability for our characters to see and hear, they will know when an enemy is nearby and when to attack.

Chapter 5, Flocking, discusses the situation where many objects travel together as a group. We will look at two different ways to implement flocking, and how it can be used to make objects move together.

Chapter 6, Path-Following and Steering Behaviors, looks at how AI characters can follow a path provided to reach a destination. Then we look at how AI characters can find a target without having a predefined path, simply by moving toward a goal while avoiding obstacles as they appear.

Chapter 7, A* Pathfinding, discusses a popular algorithm used to find the best route from a given location to a target location. With A*, we scan the terrain and find the best path that leads us to the goal.

Chapter 8, Navigation Mesh, discusses using the power of Unity to make pathfinding easier to implement. By creating a Navigation Mesh (this requires Unity Pro), we will be able to represent the scene around us in a better way than we could by using tiles and the A* algorithm.

Chapter 9, Behavior Trees, teaches you about behavior trees, a popular decision-making technique for game AI. We will explore the general architecture of behavior trees and how to use them to control a simple agent. Then we will use the free plugin *Behavior Bricks* to apply our new knowledge to a simple mini-game project.

Chapter 10, Procedural Content Generation, explores the basics of generative AI and procedural content generation. We will see how to use Perlin noise to generate realistic terrain, and how to use Cellular Automata to generate a cave-like dungeon map.

Chapter 11, Machine Learning in Unity, explores how to apply machine learning (in particular, reinforcement learning) to game characters for games or simulations. We will use the official Unity ML-Agents Toolkit. In the first part, we will learn how to configure Unity and the external requirements for the toolkit. Then we will showcase two simple practical examples.

Chapter 12, Putting It All Together, takes various elements of what you have learned throughout the book and brings it all together into one last project. Here, you will apply the remaining AI elements you have learned and create an impressive vehicle battle game.

To get the most out of this book

For this book, you only need to install a recent version of Unity3D. The code projects in this book have been tested on macOS and Windows on Unity 2022 and Unity 2021 but, with minor adjustments, they should work with future releases too.

Software/hardware covered in the book	Operating system requirements
Unity 2022	Windows 7 SP1+, 8, 10, 64-bit versions only; macOS 10.12+; Ubuntu 16.04, 18.04, and CentOS 7

For *Chapter 9, Behavior Trees,* you will need to install the Behavior Bricks plugin for Unity. In *Chapter 11, Machine Learning in Unity,* we will install Python 3.7 and PyTorch.

If you are using the digital version of this book, we advise you to type the code yourself or access the code from the book's GitHub repository (a link is available in the next section). Doing so will help you avoid any potential errors related to the copying and pasting of code.

Download the example code files

You can download the example code files for this book from GitHub at `https://github.com/PacktPublishing/Unity-Artificial-Intelligence-Programming-Fifth-Edition`. If there's an update to the code, it will be updated in the GitHub repository.

We also have other code bundles from our rich catalog of books and videos available at `https://github.com/PacktPublishing/`. Check them out!

Download the color images

We also provide a PDF file that has color images of the screenshots and diagrams used in this book. You can download it here: `https://static.packt-cdn.com/downloads/9781803238531_ColorImages.pdf`.

Conventions used

There are a number of text conventions used throughout this book.

`Code in text`: Indicates code words in text, database table names, folder names, filenames, file extensions, pathnames, dummy URLs, user input, and Twitter handles. Here is an example: "Let's start creating the `PlayerTankController` class by setting up the `Start` function and the `Update` function in the `PlayerTankController.cs` file."

A block of code is set as follows:

```
public class PlayerTankController : MonoBehaviour {
    public GameObject Bullet;
    public GameObject Turret;
    public GameObject bulletSpawnPoint;
```

When we wish to draw your attention to a particular part of a code block, the relevant lines or items are set in bold:

```
// ...
    private AudioSource m_ExplosionAudio
    private ParticleSystem m_ExplosionParticles
    private float m_CurrentHealth;
    private bool m_Dead;
    public float CurrentHealth { get; }
    // ...
```

Any command-line input or output is written as follows:

```
git clone --branch release_19 https://github.com/Unity-
Technologies/ml-agents.git
```

Bold: Indicates a new term, an important word, or words that you see onscreen. For instance, words in menus or dialog boxes appear in **bold**. Here is an example: "If you play the scene and click on the **Pull Lever** button, you should see the final result."

> Tips or important notes
> Appear like this.

Get in touch

Feedback from our readers is always welcome.

General feedback: If you have questions about any aspect of this book, email us at customercare@packtpub.com and mention the book title in the subject of your message.

Errata: Although we have taken every care to ensure the accuracy of our content, mistakes do happen. If you have found a mistake in this book, we would be grateful if you would report this to us. Please visit www.packtpub.com/support/errata and fill in the form.

Piracy: If you come across any illegal copies of our works in any form on the internet, we would be grateful if you would provide us with the location address or website name. Please contact us at copyright@packt.com with a link to the material.

If you are interested in becoming an author: If there is a topic that you have expertise in and you are interested in either writing or contributing to a book, please visit authors.packtpub.com.

Share Your Thoughts

Once you've read *Unity Artificial Intelligence Programming – Fifth Edition*, we'd love to hear your thoughts! Scan the QR code below to go straight to the Amazon review page for this book and share your feedback.

https://www.amazon.in/review/1803238534

Your review is important to us and the tech community and will help us make sure we're delivering excellent quality content.

Part 1: Basic AI

In this part, we will learn the goals of game AI and the basic techniques to implement simple but effective AI characters in game.

We will cover the following chapters in this part:

- *Chapter 1, Introduction to AI*
- *Chapter 2, Finite State Machines*
- *Chapter 3, Randomness and Probability*
- *Chapter 4, Implementing Sensors*

1
Introduction to AI

This book aims to teach you the basics of **artificial intelligence** (**AI**) programming for video games using one of the most popular commercial game engines available: Unity3D. In the upcoming chapters, you will learn how to implement many of the foundational techniques of any modern game, such as behavior trees and finite state machines.

Before that, though, you must have a little background on AI in terms of its broader, academic, traditional domain, which we will provide in this introductory chapter. Then, we'll learn how the applications and implementations of AI in games are different from other domains and the essential and unique requirements for AI in games. Finally, we'll explore the basic techniques of AI that are used in games.

In this chapter, we'll cover the following topics:

- Understanding AI
- AI in video games
- AI techniques for video games

Understanding AI

Intelligence is a natural and necessary aspect of life for all living organisms, such as animals and humans. Without intelligence – mentioned in the broadest way possible here – animals would not be able to look for food, bees would not be able to find flowers, and we humans would have never been able to craft objects or light fires, let alone develop games in Unity! On the contrary, computers are just electronic devices that can accept data, perform logical and mathematical operations at high speeds, and output the results. They lack any kind of intelligence. Computers would stay still and lifeless forever like rocks without someone telling them what to do and how to do it.

From this point of view, AI is essentially the field that studies how to give machines the spark of natural intelligence. It's a discipline that teaches computers how to think and decide like living organisms to achieve any goal without human intervention.

As you can imagine, this is a vast subject. There's no way that such a small book will be able to cover everything related to AI. Fortunately, for the goal of game AI, we do not need a comprehensive knowledge of AI. We only need to grasp the basic concepts and master the basic techniques. And this is what we will do in this book.

But before we move on to game-specific techniques, let's look at some of the main research areas for AI:

- **Computer vision**: This is the ability to take visual input from visual sources – such as videos and photos – and analyze them to identify objects (object recognition), faces (face recognition), text in handwritten documents (optical character recognition), or even to reconstruct 3D models from stereoscopic images.

- **Natural Language Processing** (**NLP**): This allows a machine to read and understand human languages – that is, how we write and speak. The problem is that human languages are difficult for machines to understand. Language ambiguity is the main problem: there are many ways to say the same thing, and the same sentence can have different meanings based on the context. NLP is a significant cognitive step for machines since they need to understand the languages and expressions we use before processing them and responding accordingly. Fortunately, many datasets are available on the web to help researchers train machines for this complex task.

- **Machine learning**: This branch of AI studies how machines can learn how to perform a task using only raw data and experience, with or without human intervention. Such tasks span from identifying if a picture contains the image of a cat, to playing board games (such as the AlphaGo software, which, in 2017, was able to beat the number one ranked player of the world in the game of Go), to perfectly interpolating the faces of famous actors in our homemade videos (so-called **deepfakes**). Machine learning is a vast field that spans all other AI fields. We will talk more about it in *Chapter 11, Machine Learning in Unity*.

- **Common sense reasoning**: There is a type of knowledge that is almost innate in human beings. For instance, we trivially know that *things fall on the ground if they're not supported* or that *we cannot put a big thing into a smaller one*. However, this kind of knowledge and reasoning (also called **common sense knowledge**) is entirely undecipherable for computers. At the time of writing, nobody knows how to teach machines such trivial – for us – things. Nevertheless, it is a very active (and frustrating) research direction.

Fortunately for us, game AI has a much narrower scope. Instead, as we will see in the next section, game AI has a single but essential goal: to make the game fun to play.

AI in video games

Different from general AI, game AI only needs to provide the *illusion of intelligence*. Its goal is not to offer human-like intelligent agents but characters that are smart enough to make a game fun to play.

Of course, making a game *fun to play* is no trivial matter, and to be fair, a good AI is just one part of the problem. Nevertheless, if a good AI is not enough to make a game *fun*, a bad AI can undermine even the most well-designed game. If you are interested in the problem of *what makes a game fun*, I suggest that you read a good book on game design, such as *The Art of Game Design*, by Jesse Schell.

However, for what concerns us, it is sufficient to say that it's essential to provide an adequate level of challenge to the player. A fair challenge, in this case, means the game should not be so difficult that the player can't beat the opponent, nor too easy that winning becomes a tedious task. Thus, finding the right challenge level is the key to making a game fun to play.

And that's where AI kicks in. The role of AI in games is to make it fun by providing challenging opponents and interesting **Non-Player Characters** (**NPCs**) that behave appropriately in the game world. So, the objective here is not to replicate the whole thought process of humans or animals but to make the NPCs seem intelligent by reacting to the changing situations in the game world so that they make sense to the player. This, as we mentioned previously, provides the illusion of intelligence.

Information

It is essential to mention that AI in games is not limited to modeling NPC's behaviors. AI is also used to generate game content (as we will see in *Chapter 10, Procedural Content Generation*) to control the story events and the narrative pace (a notable example is given by the AI director in the *Left 4 Dead* series) or even to invent entire narrative arcs.

Note that a good game AI doesn't need to be a complex AI. A recurring example is the AI of the original *Pac-Man* arcade game. By any modern standard, the algorithm that governs the behavior of the four ghosts chasing Pac-Man can barely be considered AI. Each ghost uses a really simple rule to decide where to move next: measure the distance between the ghost and a *target tile* and choose the direction to minimize the distance.

The *target tile* might be the location of Pac-Man itself (as in the case of the Red Ghost), but it can also be something in front of Pac-Man (such as the Pink Ghost) or some other tile. By simply changing the target tile's position, the Pac-Man arcade game can give each ghost a distinctive personality and an AI that challenges us even after 40 years!

The golden rule is to use the smallest amount of AI necessary to achieve the game's design goal. Of course, we may take this rule to the extreme and use no AI if we find out that it is unnecessary. For instance, in *Portal* and *Portal 2*, all the characters are completely scripted and there is no AI involved, yet nobody complained about the lack of AI.

Information

If you are interested in diving deeper into the Pac-Man AI, I suggest that you watch this very detailed video from the *Retro Game Mechanics Explained* YouTube channel: `https://www.youtube.com/watch?v=ataGotQ7ir8`.

Alternatively, if you prefer to read, you can go to this very informative web page: `https://gameinternals.com/understanding-pac-man-ghost-behavior`.

Another challenge for game AI is that other operations, such as graphics rendering and physics simulation, need to share the processing power that's required for AI. And don't forget that they are all happening in real time, so it's critical to achieve a steady frame rate throughout the game. This means that game AI needs to be designed to not overtake the computational resources. This is usually done by designing an algorithm that can be interrupted and spread over multiple frames.

In general AI, many companies invest in a dedicated processor for AI calculations called an AI accelerator (such as Google's Tensor Processing Unit). However, until games have widespread access to such dedicated AI processors, we game AI developers still need to pay attention to our algorithms' performance.

The next section will provide a general introduction to the most popular AI techniques that are used in video games.

AI techniques for video games

In this section, we will look at some of the AI techniques that are commonly used in different types of games. We'll learn how to implement each of these features in Unity in the upcoming chapters. Since this book does not focus on AI techniques themselves but on implementing these techniques inside Unity, we won't look at them in too much detail here. So, let's just take this as a crash course before diving into the implementation details.

If you want to learn more about AI for games, there are some great books, such as *Programming Game AI by Example*, by Mat Buckland, and *Artificial Intelligence for Games*, by Ian Millington and John Funge. In addition, the *AI Game Programming Wisdom and Game AI Pro* series also contain a lot of valuable resources and articles on the latest AI techniques.

Finite state machines

Finite State Machines (**FSMs**) are probably one of the simplest, most used, and most discussed AI models and, for most games, they represent the only AI technique. A state machine consists of a finite number of **states** that are connected by one or more **transitions**, resulting in a data structure known as a **graph**. Each game entity starts with an initial state. Then, environment events trigger specific rules that will make the entity move into another state. Such triggering rules are called **transitions**. A game entity can only be in one state at any given time.

For example, let's consider an AI guard character in a typical shooting game. Its states could be as simple as *patrolling*, *chasing*, and *shooting*:

Figure 1.1 – A simple FSM for an AI guard character

There are four components in a simple FSM:

- **States**: This component defines a set of states that a game entity or an NPC can choose from (**Patrol**, **Chase**, and **Shoot**).

- **Transitions**: This component defines the relationships between different states.

- **Rules**: This component defines when to perform a state transition (**Player in sight**, **Close enough to attack**, and **Lost/killed player**).

- **Events**: This is the component that will trigger to check the rules (the guard's visible area, distance to the player, and so on).

So, a monster in *Quake 2* may have the following states: standing, walking, running, dodging, attacking, idle, and searching.

FSMs are widely used in games because they are simple to implement using only a bunch of *if* or *switch* statements, but they are still powerful enough for simple and somewhat complex games. On the other hand, they can get messy when we need a lot of states and transitions. We'll learn how to manage a simple FSM in the next chapter.

Randomness and probability in AI

Imagine an enemy bot in a **First-Person Shooter** (**FPS**) game that can always kill the player with a headshot or an opponent in a racing game who always chooses the best route and never collides with any obstacle. Such a level of *intelligence* will make the game so hard that it will become almost impossible to win and, as a consequence, it will be frustrating to play. On the opposite side of the spectrum, imagine an enemy that chooses the same predictable route whenever it tries to escape from the player. After a couple of games, the player will learn the enemy's pattern, and the game will feel boring. AI-controlled entities that behave the same way every time the player encounters them make the game predictable, easy to win, and therefore dull.

Of course, there are some cases in which *intentional predictability* is a desired feature. In stealth games, for instance, we want the players to be able to predict the path of the enemies so that the players can plan a sneaking route. But in other cases, *unintentional predictability* can interfere with the game's engagement and make the player feel like the game is not challenging or fair enough. One way to fix these *too-perfect* or *too-stupid* AIs is to introduce intentional mistakes in their behavior. In games, we introduce randomness and probability in the decision-making process of AI calculations.

There are multiple scenarios where we may want to introduce a bit of randomness. The most straightforward case is when the NPC has no information and/or it doesn't matter what decision it makes. For instance, in a shooting game, an enemy under fire may want to decide where to cover. So, instead of always moving it to the closest cover, we may wish to instruct the NPCs to sometimes choose a slightly far-away cover.

In other cases, we can use randomness for the outcomes of a decision. For example, we can use randomness for hit probabilities, add or subtract random bits of damage to/from base damage, or make an NPC hesitate before they start shooting.

The sensor system

Our AI characters need to know their surroundings and the world they interact with to make a particular decision. Such information includes the following:

- **The position of the player**: This is used to decide whether to attack or chase or keep patrolling.
- **Buildings and nearby objects**: This is used to hide or take cover.

- **The player's health and the AI's health**: This is used to decide whether to retreat or advance.

- **Location of resources on the map in a Real-Time Strategy (RTS) game**: This is used to occupy and collect resources that are required to update and/or produce other units.

As you can imagine, choosing the correct method to collect game information can vary a lot, depending on the type of game we are trying to build. In the next few sections, we'll look at two basic strategies: **polling** and **message (event) systems**.

Polling

One method to collect such information is **polling**. Polling consists of directly checking for the preceding information in Unity's `FixedUpdate` method of our AI character. In this way, AI characters can just poll the information they are interested in from the game world, do the checks, and take action accordingly. Polling works great if there aren't too many things to check.

To make this method more efficient, we may want to program the characters to poll the world states at different rates so that we do not have all the characters checking everything at once. For instance, we may divide the polling agents into 10 groups (G1, G2, G3, and so on) and assign the polling for each group at different frames (for example, G1 will poll at frame 0, 60, 120, and so on; G2 will poll at frame 10, 70, 130, and so on).

As another example, we may decide to change the polling frequency based on the enemy's type or state. For instance, enemies that are disengaged and far away may poll every 3-4 seconds, while enemies closer to the player and under attack may want to poll every 0.5 seconds.

However, polling is no longer enough as soon as the game gets bigger. Therefore, in more massive games with more complex AI systems, we need to implement an event-driven method using a global messaging system.

Messaging systems

In a messaging system, the game communicates events between the AI entity and the player, the world, or the other AI entities through asynchronous messages. For example, when the player attacks an enemy unit inside a group of patrol guards, the other AI units need to know about this incident so that they can start searching for and attacking the player.

If we were using the polling method, our AI entities would need to check the state of all of the other AI entities to find out if one of them has been attacked. However, we can implement this in a more manageable and scalable fashion: we can register the AI characters that are interested in a particular event as listeners of that event; then, if that event occurs, our messaging system will broadcast this information to all listeners. The AI entities can then take the appropriate actions or perform further checks.

This event-driven system does not necessarily provide a faster mechanism than polling. Still, it provides a convenient, central checking system that senses the world and informs the interested AI agents, rather than having each agent check the same event in every frame. In reality, both polling and messaging systems are used together most of the time. For example, the AI may poll for more detailed information when it receives an event from the messaging system.

Flocking, swarming, and herding

Many living beings such as birds, fish, insects, and land animals perform specific operations such as moving, hunting, and foraging in groups. They stay and hunt in groups because it makes them stronger and safer from predators than pursuing goals individually. So, let's say you want a group of birds flocking, swarming around in the sky; it'll cost too much time and effort for animators to design the movement and animations of each bird. However, if we apply some simple rules for each bird to follow, we can achieve an emergent intelligence for the whole group with complex, global behavior.

One pioneer of this concept is Craig Reynolds, who presented such a flocking algorithm in his 1987 SIGGRAPH paper, *Flocks, Herds, and Schools – A Distributed Behavioral Model*. He coined the term **boid**, which sounds like "bird" but refers to a bird-like object. He proposed three simple rules to apply to each unit:

- **Separation**: Each boid needs to maintain a minimum distance from neighboring boids to avoid hitting them (short-range repulsion).

- **Alignment**: Each boid needs to align itself with the average direction of its neighbors and then move in the same velocity with them as a flock.

- **Cohesion**: Each boid is attracted to the group's center of mass (long-range attraction).

These three simple rules are all we need to implement a realistic and reasonably complex flocking behavior for birds. This doesn't only work with birds. Flocking behaviors are useful for modeling a crowd or even a couple of NPCs that will follow the player during the game.

We'll learn how to implement such a flocking system in Unity in *Chapter 5, Flocking*.

Path following and steering

Sometimes, we want our AI characters to roam the game world and follow a roughly guided or thoroughly defined path. For example, in a racing game, the AI opponents need to navigate a road. In that case, simple reactive algorithms, such as our flocking boid algorithm, are not powerful enough to solve this problem. Still, in the end, it all comes down to dealing with actual movements and steering behaviors. Steering behaviors for AI characters has been a research topic for a couple of decades now.

One notable paper in this field is *Steering Behaviors for Autonomous Characters*, again by Craig Reynolds, presented in 1999 at the **Game Developers Conference** (**GDC**). He categorized steering behaviors into the following three layers:

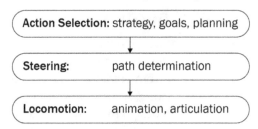

Figure 1.2 – Hierarchy of motion behaviors

To understand these layers, let's look at an example. Imagine that you are working at your desk on a hot summer afternoon. You are thirsty, and you want a cold glass of iced tea. So, we start from the first layer: we want a cold glass of iced tea (setting the goal), and we plan out what we need to do to get it. We probably need to go to the kitchen (unless you have a mini-fridge under your desk), fetch an empty glass, and then move to the fridge, open it, and get the iced tea (we have made a high-level plan).

Now, we move to the second layer. Unless your kitchen is a direct straight line from your desk, you need to determine a path: go around the desk, move through a corridor, navigate around the kitchen furniture until you reach the cabinet with the glasses, and so on. Now that you have a path, it is time to move to the third layer: walking the path. In this example, the third layer is represented by your body, skeleton, and muscles moving you along the path.

> **Information**
>
> Don't worry – you don't need to master all three layers. As an AI programmer, you only need to focus on the first two. The third layer is usually handled by graphic programmers – in particular, animators.

After describing these three layers, Craig Reynolds explains how to design and implement standard steering behaviors for individual AI characters. Such behaviors include *seek* and *flee*, *pursue* and *evade*, *wander*, *arrival*, *obstacle avoidance*, *wall following*, and *path following*.

We'll implement some of these behaviors in Unity in *Chapter 6, Path Following and Steering Behaviors*.

A* pathfinding

There are many games where you can find monsters or enemies that follow the player or move to a particular point while avoiding obstacles. For example, let's take a look at a typical RTS game. You can select a group of units and click a location where you want them to move or click on the enemy units to attack them.

Then, your units need to find a way to reach the goal without colliding with the obstacles. Of course, the enemy units also need to be able to do the same. The barriers could be different for different units. For example, an airforce unit may pass over a mountain, while the ground or artillery units need to find a way around it.

A* (pronounced *A-star*) is a pathfinding algorithm that's widely used in games because of its performance, accuracy, and ease of implementation. Let's look at an example to see how it works. Let's say we want our unit to move from point **A** to point **B**, but there's a wall in the way, and it can't go straight toward the target. So, it needs to find a way to point **B** while avoiding the wall:

Figure 1.3 – Top-down view of our map

This is a simple 2D example, but we can apply the same idea to 3D environments. To find the path from point **A** to point **B**, we need to know more about the map, such as the position of obstacles. For that, we can split our whole map into small tiles that represent the entire map in a grid format, as shown in the following diagram:

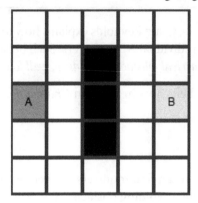

Figure 1.4 – Map represented in a 2D grid

The tiles can also be of other shapes, such as hexagons or triangles. Each shape comes with its advantages. For instance, hexagonal tiles are convenient because they do not have the problem of *diagonal moves* (all the hexagons surrounding a target hexagon are at the same distance). In this example, though, we have used square tiles because they are the more intuitive shape that comes to mind when we think about **grids**.

Now, we can reference our map in a small 2D array.

We can represent our map with a 5x5 grid of square tiles for a total of 25 tiles. Now, we can start searching for the best path to reach the target. How do we do this? By calculating the movement score of each tile that's adjacent to the starting tile that is not occupied by an obstacle, and then choosing the tile with the lowest cost.

If we don't consider the diagonal movements, there are four possible adjacent tiles to the player. Now, we need to use two numbers to calculate the movement score for each of those tiles. Let's call them G and H, where G is the cost to move from the starting tile to the current tile, and H is the estimated cost to reach the target tile from the current tile.

Let's call F the sum of G and H, ($F = G + H$) – that is, the final score of that tile:

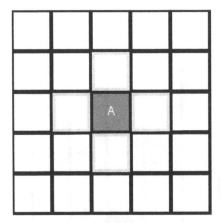

Figure 1.5 – Valid adjacent tiles

In our example, to estimate *H*, we'll use a simple method called **Manhattan length** (also known as **taxicab geometry**). According to this method, the distance (cost) between **A** and **B** is the number of horizontal tiles, **A** and **B**, plus the number of vertical tiles between **A** and **B**:

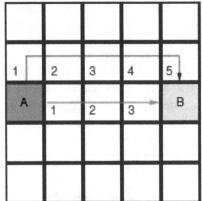

Figure 1.6 – Calculating G

The *G* value, on the other hand, represents the *cost so far* during the search. The preceding diagram shows the calculations of *G* with two different paths. To compute the current *G*, we must add 1 (the cost of moving one tile) to the previous tile's *G* score. However, we can give different costs to different tiles. For example, we may want to set a higher movement cost for diagonal movements (if we are considering them) or, for instance, to tiles occupied by a pond or a muddy road.

Now that we know how to get *G*, let's learn how to calculate *H*. The following diagram shows the *H* value for different starting tiles. Even in this case, we use the Manhattan distance:

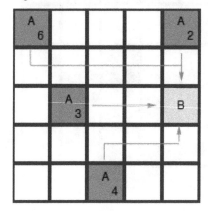

Figure 1.7 – Calculating H

So, now that we know how to get *G* and *H*, let's go back to our original example to figure out the shortest path from **A** to **B**. First, we must choose the starting tile and collect all its adjacent tiles, as shown in the following diagram. Then, we must calculate each tile's *G* and *H* scores, as shown in the tile's lower left and right corners. Finally, we must get the final score, *F*, by adding *G* and *H* together. You can see the *F* score in the tile's top-left corner.

Now, we must choose the tile with the lowest *F* score as our next tile and store the previous tile as its parent. Note that keeping records of each tile's parents is crucial because we will use this backlink later to trace the sequence of nodes from the end to the start to obtain the final path. In this example, we must choose the tile to the right of the starting position and consider it the current tile:

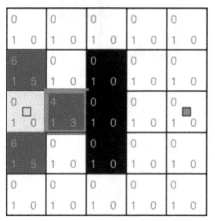

Figure 1.8 – Starting position

From the current tile, we repeat this process, starting with collecting the valid adjacent tiles. There are only two free adjacent tiles this time: the one above the current tile and the one at the bottom (in fact, the left tile is the starting tile – which we've already examined – and the obstacle occupies the right tile). We calculate G and H, and then the F score of those new adjacent tiles.

This time, we have four tiles on our map, all with the same score: six. Therefore, we can choose any of them. In fact, in the end, we will find the shortest path independently of which tile we explore first (proving the math behind this statement is outside the scope of this book):

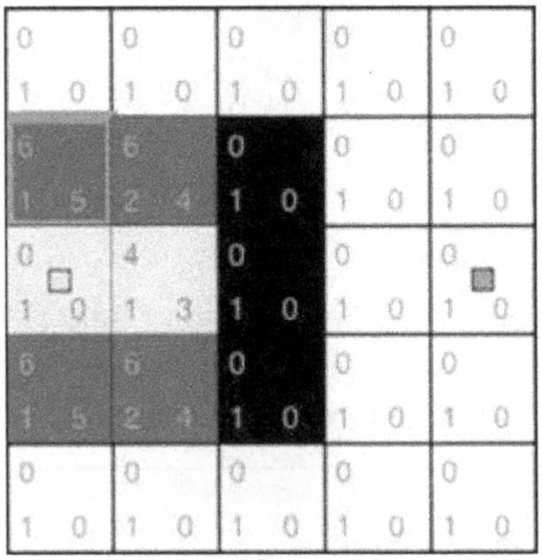

Figure 1.9 – Second step

In this example, from the group of tiles with a cost of 6, we chose the tile at the top left as the starting position. Again, we must examine the adjacent tiles. In this step, there's only one new adjacent tile with a calculated F score of 8. Because the lowest score is still 6 right now, we can choose any tile with a score of 6:

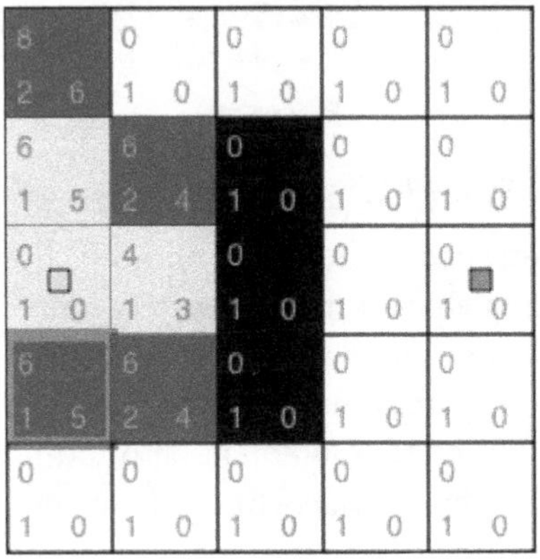

Figure 1.10 – Third step

If we repeat this process until we reach our target tile, we'll end up with a board that shows all the scores for each free tile:

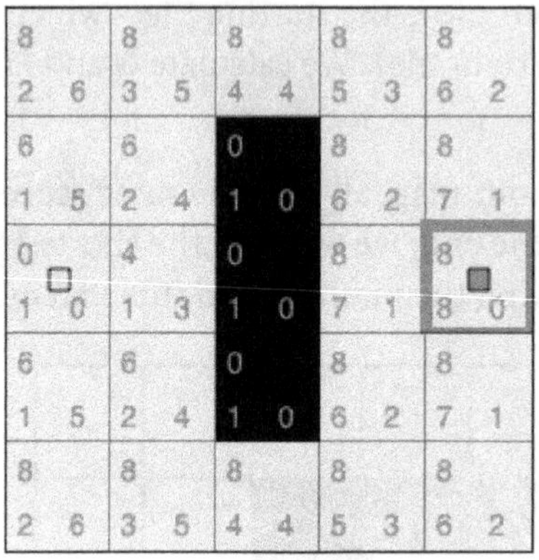

Figure 1.11 – Reach target

There is only one step left. Do you remember the parent links that we stored in each node? Now, starting from the target tile, we must use the stored parent tile to trace back a list of tiles. The resulting list will be a path that looks something like this:

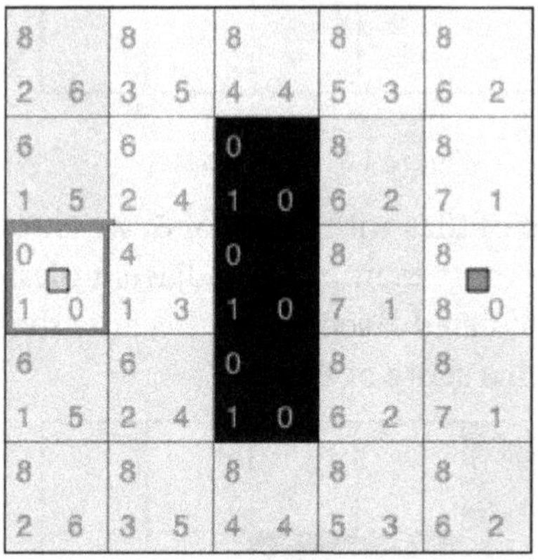

Figure 1.12 – Path traced back

What we explained here is the essence of the A* pathfinding algorithm, which is the basic founding block of any pathfinding algorithm. Fortunately, since Unity 3.5, a couple of new features such as automatic navigation mesh generation and the NavMesh Agent make implementing pathfinding in your games much more accessible. As a result, you may not even need to know anything about A* to implement pathfinding for your AI characters. Nonetheless, knowing how the system works behind the scenes is essential to becoming a solid AI programmer.

We'll talk about NavMesh in the next section and then in more detail in *Chapter 8, Navigation Mesh*.

Navigation meshes

Now that you know the basics of the A* pathfinding algorithm, you may notice that using a grid in A* requires many steps to get the shortest path between the start and target position. It may not seem notable but searching for a path tile-by-tile for huge maps with thousands of mostly empty tiles is a severe waste of computational power. So, games often use waypoints as a guide to move the AI characters as a simple and effective way to use fewer computation resources.

Let's say we want to move our AI character from point **A** to point **B**, and we've set up three waypoints, as shown in the following diagram:

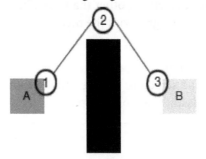

Figure 1.13 – Waypoints

All we have to do now is apply the A* algorithm to the waypoints (there are fewer of these compared to the number of tiles) and then simply move the character in a straight line from waypoint to waypoint.

However, waypoints are not without issues. What if we want to update the obstacles in our map? We'll have to place the waypoints again for the updated map, as shown in the following diagram:

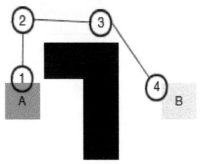

Figure 1.14 – New waypoints

Moreover, following each node to the target produces characters that look unrealistic. For instance, they move in straight lines, followed by an abrupt change of direction, much like the mechanical puppets in a theme park's attraction. Or the path that connects two waypoints may be too close to the obstacles. For example, look at the preceding diagrams; the AI character will likely collide with the wall where the path is close to the wall.

If that happens, our AI will keep trying to go through the wall to reach the next target, but it won't be able to, and it will get stuck there. Sure, we could make the path more realistic by smoothing out the zigzag path using splines, or we could manually check each path to avoid grazing the edges of obstacles. However, the problem is that the waypoints don't contain any information about the environment other than the trajectory that's connecting two nodes.

To address such situations, we're going to need a tremendous number of waypoints, which are very hard to manage. So, for everything other than straightforward games, we must exchange the computational cost of a grid with the mental and design cost of managing hundreds of waypoints.

Fortunately, there is a better solution: using a navigation mesh. A **navigation mesh** (often called **NavMesh**) is another graph structure that we can use to represent our world, similar to square tile-based grids and waypoint graphs:

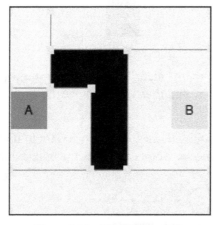

Figure 1.15 – Navigation mesh

A NavMesh uses convex polygons to represent the areas in the map where an AI entity can travel. The most crucial benefit of using a NavMesh is that it contains much more information about the environment than a waypoint system. With a NavMesh, we can automatically adjust our path safely because we know that our AI entities can move freely inside a region. Another advantage of using a NavMesh is that we can use the same mesh for different types of AI entities. Different AI entities can have different properties such as size, speed, and movement abilities. For instance, a set of waypoints may be suitable for human characters, but they may not work nicely for flying creatures or AI-controlled vehicles. Those may need different sets of waypoints (with all the problems that this adds).

However, programmatically generating a NavMesh based on a scene is a somewhat complicated process. Fortunately, Unity includes a built-in NavMesh generator.

Since this is not a book on core AI techniques, we won't go into how to generate such NavMeshes. Instead, we'll learn how to efficiently use Unity's NavMesh to implement pathfinding for our AI characters.

Behavior trees

Behavior trees are another technique that's used to represent and control the logic behind AI characters' decisions. They have become popular for their applications in AAA games such as *Halo* and *Spore*. We briefly covered FSMs earlier in this chapter, which is a straightforward way to define the logic of AI characters based on the transition between different states in reaction to game events. However, FSMs have two main issues: they are challenging to scale and reuse.

To support all the scenarios where we want our characters to be, we need to add a lot of states and hardwire many transitions. So, we need something that scales better with more extensive problems. Behavior trees represent a sensible step in the right direction.

As its name suggests, the essence of a behavior tree is a tree-like data structure. The leaves of such trees are called **tasks**, and they represent our character's actions (for instance, *attack, chase, patrol, hide*, and so on) or sensory input (for example, *Is the player near?* or *Am I close enough to attack?*). Instead, the internal nodes of the trees are represented by control flow nodes, which guide the execution of the tree. **Sequence**, **Selector**, and **Parallel Decorator** are commonly used control flow nodes.

Now, let's try to reimplement the example from the *Finite state machines* section using a behavior tree. First, we can break all the transitions and states into basic tasks:

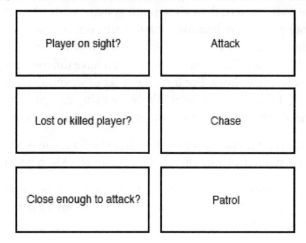

Figure 1.16 – Tasks

Now, let's look at a Selector node. We represent a Selector with a circle with a question mark inside it. When executed, a Selector node tries to execute all the child tasks/sub-trees in sequential order until the first one that returns with success. In other words, if we have a Selector with four children (for example, A, B, C, and D), the Selector node executes A first. If A fails, then the Selector executes B. If B fails, then it executes C, and so on. If *any* of the tasks return a Success, then the Sequence returns a Success as soon as that task completes.

In the following example, the Selector node first chooses to attack the player. If the **Attack** task returns a Success (that is, if the player is in attack range), the Selector node stops the execution and returns with a Success to its parent node – if there is one. Instead, if the **Attack** task returns with a failure, the Selector node moves to the **Chase** task. Here, we repeat what we did previously: if the **Chase** task succeeds, the Selector node succeeds; if the **Chase** task fails, it tries the **Patrol** task, and so on:

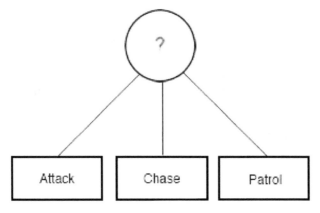

Figure 1.17 – Selector node

What about the other kind of tasks – the ones that check the game state? We use them with Sequence nodes, which are usually represented with a rectangle with an arrow inside them. A Sequence node is similar to a Selector node with a crucial difference: it only returns a Success message if *every* sub-tree returns with a Success. In other words, if we have a Sequence with four children (for example, A, B, C, and D), the Sequence node will execute A, then B, then C, and finally D. If *all* the tasks return a Success, then the Sequence returns a Success.

In the following example, the first Sequence node checks whether the player character is close enough to attack. If this task succeeds, it will proceed to the next task: attacking the player. If the **Attack** task also returns with a Success message, the whole Sequence terminates with success. Instead, if the **Close Enough to Attack?** task fails, then the Sequence node does not proceed to the **Attack** task and returns a failed status to the parent Selector node. Then, the Selector chooses the next task in the Sequence, **Lost or Killed Player**, and the execution continues:

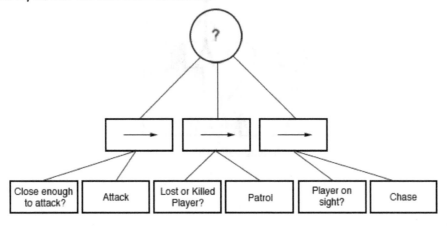

Figure 1.18 – Sequence tasks

The other two common nodes are **Parallel** and **Decorator**. A Parallel node executes all of its child tasks simultaneously (while the Sequence and Selector nodes only execute their child trees one by one). A Decorator is another type of node that has only one child. It is used to change the behavior of its own single child's sub-tree, for instance, to run it multiple times or invert the subtree's result (if the subtree returns a Success message, the decorator returns a failure, and vice versa).

We'll learn how to implement a basic behavior tree system in Unity in *Chapter 9, Behavior Trees*.

Locomotion

Animals (including humans) have a very complex musculoskeletal system that allows them to move around their environment. Animals also have sophisticated brains that tell them how to use such a system. For instance, we instinctively know where to put our steps when climbing a ladder, stairs, or uneven terrain, and we also know how to balance our bodies to stabilize all the fancy poses we want to make. We can do all this using a brain that controls our bones, muscles, joints, and other tissues, collectively described as our locomotor system.

Now, let's put this in a game development perspective. Let's say we have a human character who needs to walk on uneven surfaces or small slopes, and we have only one animation for a walk cycle. With the lack of a locomotor system in our virtual character, this is what it would look like:

Figure 1.19 – Climbing stairs without locomotion

First, we play the walk animation and move the player forward. But now, the character is penetrating the surface. So, the collision detection system pulls the character above the surface to stop this impossible configuration.

Now, let's look at how we walk upstairs in reality. We put our foot firmly on the staircase and, using force, we pull the rest of our body onto the next step. However, it's not simple to implement this level of realism in games. We'll need many animations for different scenarios, including climbing ladders, walking/running upstairs, and so on. So, in the past, only the large studios with many animators could pull this off. Nowadays, however, we have automated systems for this:

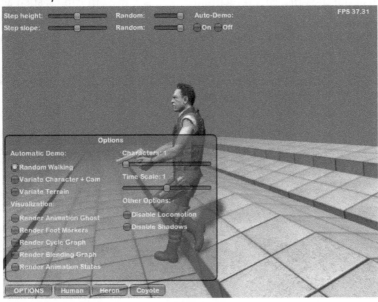

Figure 1.20 – Unity extension for inverse kinematics

This system can automatically blend our animated walk/run cycles and adjust the movements of the bones in the player's legs to ensure that the player's feet step on the ground correctly (in literature, this is called **inverse kinematics**). It can also adjust the animations that were initially designed for a specific speed and direction, to any speed and direction on any surface, such as steps and slopes. In *Chapter 6, Path Following and Steering Behaviors*, we'll learn how to use this locomotion system to apply realistic movement to our AI characters.

Summary

In this chapter, we learned that game AI and academic AI have different objectives. Academic AI researchers try to solve real-world problems and develop AI algorithms that compete with human intelligence, with the ultimate goal of replacing humans in complex situations. On the other hand, game AI focuses on building NPCs with limited resources that seem to be intelligent to the player, with the ultimate goal of entertaining them. The objective of AI in games is to provide a challenging opponent that makes the game more fun to play.

We also learned about the different AI techniques that are used in games, such as FSMs, randomness and probability, sensors, input systems, flocking and group behaviors, path following and steering behaviors, AI pathfinding, navigation mesh generation, and behavior trees.

We'll learn how to implement these techniques inside the Unity engine in the following chapters. In the next chapter, we will start with the basics: FSMs.

2
Finite State Machines

In this chapter, we'll learn how to implement a **Finite State Machine** (**FSM**) in a Unity3D game by studying the simple tank game-mechanic example that comes with this book.

In our game, the player controls a tank. The enemy tanks move around the scene, following four waypoints. Once the player's tank enters the vision range of the enemy tanks, they start chasing it; then, once they are close enough to attack, they'll start shooting at our player's tank.

To control the AI of our enemy tanks, we use an FSM. First, we'll use simple `switch` statements to implement our tank AI states. Then, we'll use a more complex and engineered FSM framework that will allow us greater flexibility in designing the character's FSM.

The topics we will be covering in this chapter are the following:

- Implementing the player's tank
- Implementing a bullet class
- Setting up waypoints
- Creating the abstract FSM class

- Using a simple FSM for the enemy tank AI
- Using an FSM framework

Technical requirements

For this chapter, you just need Unity3D 2022. You can find the example project described in this chapter in the `Chapter 2` folder in the book repository: `https://github.com/PacktPublishing/Unity-Artificial-Intelligence-Programming-Fifth-Edition/tree/main/Chapter02`.

Implementing the player's tank

Before writing the script for our player's tank, let's look at how we set up the **PlayerTank** game object. Our **Tank** object is a simple **mesh** with the `Rigidbody` and `Box Collider` components.

The **Tank** object is composed of two separate meshes, the **Tank** and **Turret**, with **Turret** being a child of **Tank**. This structure allows for the independent rotation of the **Turret** object using the mouse movement and, at the same time, automatically following the **Tank** body wherever it goes. Then, we create an empty game object for our **SpawnPoint** transform. We use it as a reference position point when shooting a bullet. Finally, we need to assign the **Player** tag to our **Tank** object. Now, let's take a look at the `controller` class:

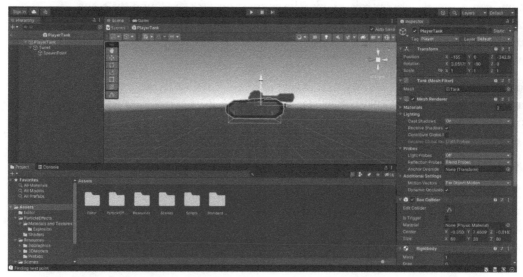

Figure 2.1 – Our tank entity

The `PlayerTankController` class controls the player's tank. We use the *W*, *A*, *S*, and *D* keys to move and steer the tank and the left mouse button to aim and shoot from the **Turret** object.

> **Information**
>
> In this book, we assume that you are using a *QWERTY* keyboard and a two-button mouse, with the left mouse button set as the primary mouse button. If you are using a different keyboard, all you have to do is pretend that you are using a *QWERTY* keyboard or try to modify the code to adapt it to your keyboard layout. It is pretty easy!

Initializing the Tank object

Let's start creating the `PlayerTankController` class by setting up the `Start` function and the `Update` function in the `PlayerTankController.cs` file:

```csharp
using UnityEngine;
using System.Collections;

public class PlayerTankController : MonoBehaviour {
    public GameObject Bullet;
    public GameObject Turret;
    public GameObject bulletSpawnPoint;

    public float rotSpeed = 150.0f;
    public float turretRotSpeed = 10.0f;
    public float maxForwardSpeed = 300.0f;
    public float maxBackwardSpeed = -300.0f;
    public float shootRate = 0.5f;

    private float curSpeed, targetSpeed;

    protected float elapsedTime;

    void Start() {
    }

    void Update() {
```

```
        UpdateWeapon();
        UpdateControl();
    }
```

We can see in the hierarchy that the **PlayerTank** game object has one child called **Turret**, and in turn, the first child of the **Turret** object is called **SpawnPoint**. To set up the controller, we need to link (by dragging and dropping) **Turret** and **SpawnPoint** into the corresponding fields in the Inspector:

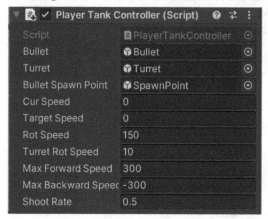

Figure 2.2 – The Player Tank Controller component in the Inspector

Later, after creating the **Bullet** object, we can assign it to the `Bullet` variable using the Inspector. Then, finally, the `Update` function calls the `UpdateControl` and `UpdateWeapon` functions. We will discuss the content of these functions in the following section.

Shooting the bullet

The mechanism for shooting the bullet is simple. Whenever the player clicks the left mouse button, we check whether the total elapsed time since the last fire is greater than the weapon's fire rate. If it is, then we create a new **Bullet** object at the `bulletSpawnPoint` transform's position. This check prevents the player from shooting a continuous stream of bullets.

For this, we add the following function to the `PlayerTankController.cs` file:

```
void UpdateWeapon() {
    elapsedTime += Time.deltaTime;
    if (Input.GetMouseButtonDown(0)) {
        if (elapsedTime >= shootRate) {
```

```
        //Reset the time
        elapsedTime = 0.0f;
        //Instantiate the bullet
        Instantiate(Bullet,
            bulletSpawnPoint.transform.position,
            bulletSpawnPoint.transform.rotation);
      }
   }
}
```

Now, we can attach this controller script to the **PlayerTank** object. If we run the game, we should be able to shoot from our tanks. Now, it is time to implement the tank's movement controls.

Controlling the tank

The player can rotate the **Turret** object using the mouse. This part may be a little bit tricky because it involves raycasting and 3D rotations. We assume that the camera looks down upon the battlefield. Let's add the `UpdateControl` function to the `PlayerTankController.cs` file:

```
void UpdateControl() {
    // AIMING WITH THE MOUSE
    // Generate a plane that intersects the Transform's
    // position with an upwards normal.
    Plane playerPlane = new Plane(Vector3.up,
        transform.position + new Vector3(0, 0, 0));

    // Generate a ray from the cursor position
    Ray RayCast =
        Camera.main.ScreenPointToRay(Input.mousePosition);

    // Determine the point where the cursor ray intersects
    // the plane.
    float HitDist = 0;

    // If the ray is parallel to the plane, Raycast will
    // return false.
```

```
if (playerPlane.Raycast(RayCast, out HitDist)) {
    // Get the point along the ray that hits the
    // calculated distance.
    Vector3 RayHitPoint = RayCast.GetPoint(HitDist);

    Quaternion targetRotation =
        Quaternion.LookRotation(RayHitPoint -
                                transform.position);

    Turret.transform.rotation = Quaternion.Slerp(
        Turret.transform.rotation, targetRotation,
        Time.deltaTime * turretRotSpeed);
}
}
```

We use raycasting to determine the turning direction by finding the mousePosition coordinates on the battlefield:

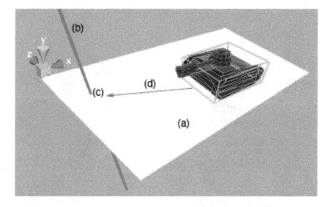

Figure 2.3 – Raycast to aim with the mouse

> **Information**
>
> **Raycasting** is a tool provided by default in the Unity physics engine. It allows us to find the intersection point between an imaginary line (the *ray*) and a collider in the scene. Imagine this as a laser pointer: we can fire our laser in a direction and see the point where it hits. However, this is a relatively expensive operation. While, in general, you can confidently handle 100–200 raycasts per frame, their performance is greatly affected by the length of the ray and the number and types of colliders in the scene. So, as a quick tip, try not to use a lot of raycasts with mesh colliders and use layer masks to filter out unnecessary colliders.

This is how it works:

1. Set up a plane that intersects with the player tank with an upward normal.
2. Shoot a ray from screen space with the mouse position (in the preceding diagram, we assume that we're looking down at the tank).
3. Find the point where the ray intersects the plane.
4. Finally, find the rotation from the current position to that intersection point.

Then, we check for the key-pressed input and move or rotate the tank accordingly. We add the following code at the end of the `UpdateControl` function:

```
if (Input.GetKey(KeyCode.W)) {
    targetSpeed = maxForwardSpeed;
} else if (Input.GetKey(KeyCode.S)) {
    targetSpeed = maxBackwardSpeed;
} else {
    targetSpeed = 0;
}


if (Input.GetKey(KeyCode.A)) {
    transform.Rotate(0, -rotSpeed * Time.deltaTime, 0.0f);
} else if (Input.GetKey(KeyCode.D)) {
    transform.Rotate(0, rotSpeed * Time.deltaTime, 0.0f);
```

```
}
```

```
//Determine current speed
curSpeed = Mathf.Lerp(curSpeed, targetSpeed, 7.0f *
                    Time.deltaTime);
transform.Translate(Vector3.forward * Time.deltaTime *
                    curSpeed);
```

The preceding code represents the classic *WASD* control scheme. The tank rotates with the *A* and *D* keys, and moves forward and backward with *W* and *S*.

Information

Depending on your level of Unity expertise, you may wonder what about the `Lerp` and `Time.deltaTime` multiplications. It may be worth a slight digression. First, **Lerp** stands for **Linear Interpolation** and is a way to transition between two values smoothly. In the preceding code, we use the `Lerp` function to smoothly spread the velocity changes over multiple frames so that the tank's movement doesn't look like it's accelerating and decelerating instantaneously. The `7.0f` value is just a *smoothing factor*, and you can play with it to find your favorite value (the bigger the value, the greater the tank's acceleration).

Then, we multiply everything by `Time.deltaTime`. This value represents the time in seconds between now and the last frame, and we use it to make our velocity independent from the frame rate. For more info, refer to `https://learn.unity.com/tutorial/delta-time`.

Next, it is time to implement the projectiles fired by the player and enemy tanks.

Implementing a Bullet class

Next, we set up our **Bullet** prefab with two orthogonal planes and a box collider, using a laser-like material and a **Particles/Additive-Layer** property in the **Shader** field:

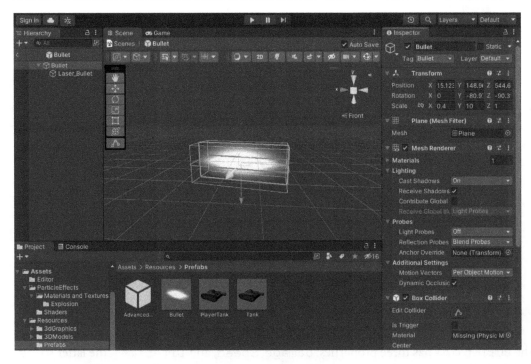

Figure 2.4 – Our Bullet prefab

The code in the Bullet.cs file is as follows:

```
using UnityEngine;
using System.Collections;

public class Bullet : MonoBehaviour {
    //Explosion Effect
    [SerializeField] // Used to expose in the inspector private
                     // fields!
    private GameObject Explosion;
    [SerializeField]
    private float Speed = 600.0f;
    [SerializeField]
    private float LifeTime = 3.0f;
    public int damage = 50;
```

```
    void Start() {
        Destroy(gameObject, LifeTime);
    }

    void Update() {
        transform.position +=
        transform.forward * Speed * Time.deltaTime;
    }

    void OnCollisionEnter(Collision collision) {
        ContactPoint contact = collision.contacts[0];
        Instantiate(Explosion, contact.point,
                    Quaternion.identity);
        Destroy(gameObject);
    }
}
```

The Bullet class has three properties: damage, Speed, and Lifetime – the latter so that the bullet is automatically destroyed after a certain amount of time. Note that we use [SerializeField] to show the private fields in the Inspector; by default, in fact, Unity only shows public fields. It is a good practice to set fields that we need to access from other classes as public-only.

As you can see, the Explosion property of the bullet is linked to the ParticleExplosion prefab, which we're not going to discuss in detail. This prefab is in the ParticleEffects folder, so we drop it into the **Shader** field. Then, when the bullet hits something, we play this particle effect, as described in the OnCollisionEnter method. The ParticleExplosion prefab uses the AutoDestruct script to automatically destroy the Explosion object after a small amount of time:

```
using UnityEngine;

public class AutoDestruct : MonoBehaviour {
    [SerializeField]
    private float DestructTime = 2.0f;
```

```
    void Start() {
        Destroy(gameObject, DestructTime);
    }
}
```

The `AutoDestruct` script is small but convenient. It just destroys the attached object after a certain number of seconds. Many Unity games use a similar script almost every time for many situations.

Now that we have a tank that can fire and move, we can set up a simple patrolling path for the enemy tanks.

Setting up waypoints

By default, the enemy tanks will patrol the game arena. To implement this behavior, we need to specify first the patrolling path. We will explore path following thoroughly in *Chapter 6, Path Following and Steering Behaviors*. For now, we limit ourselves to a simple *waypoints path*.

To implement it, we put four **Cube** game objects at random places. They represent *waypoints* inside our scene, and therefore, we name each one `WanderPoint`:

Figure 2.5 – WanderPoint

Here is what our **WanderPoint** objects look like:

Figure 2.6 – The WanderPoint properties

Note that we need to tag these points with a tag called **WanderPoint**. Later, we will use this tag when we try to find the waypoints from our tank AI. As you can see in its properties, a waypoint is just a **Cube** game object with the **Mesh Renderer** checkbox disabled:

Figure 2.7 – The gizmo selection panel

To show these points in the editor (but not in the game), we use an empty object with a gizmo icon, since all we need from a waypoint is its position and the transformation data. To do that, click the small triangle near the object icon in the Inspector, as shown in *Figure 2.7*.

We are now ready to give life to the enemy tanks with the power of the FSM.

Creating the abstract FSM class

Next, we implement a generic abstract class to define the enemy tank AI class's methods. This abstract class will be the skeleton of our AI and represent a high-level view of what an enemy tank should do.

We can see the code of this class in the FSM.cs file:

```
using UnityEngine;
using System.Collections;

public class FSM : MonoBehaviour {
    protected virtual void Initialize() { }

    protected virtual void FSMUpdate() { }

    protected virtual void FSMFixedUpdate() { }

    // Use this for initialization
    void Start () {
        Initialize();
    }

    // Update is called once per frame
    void Update () {
        FSMUpdate();
    }

    void FixedUpdate() {
        FSMFixedUpdate();
    }
}
```

The enemy tanks need only to know the position of the player's tank, their next destination point, and the list of waypoints to choose from while they're patrolling. Once the player tank is in range, they rotate their turret object and start shooting from the bullet spawn point at their fire rate.

As we explained before, we will extend this class in two ways: using a simple *if-then-else*-based FSM (the `SimpleFSM` class) and a more engineered but more flexible FSM (`AdvancedFSM`). These two FSM implementations will inherit the `FSM` abstract class, and they will implement the three abstract methods: `Initialize`, `FSMUpdate`, and `FSMFixedUpdate`.

We will see the two different ways to implement these three methods in the next sections. For now, let's start with the basic implementation.

Using a simple FSM for the enemy tank AI

Let's look at the actual code for our AI tanks. First, let's create a new class, called `SimpleFSM`, which inherits from our FSM abstract class.

You can find the source code in the `SimpleFSM.cs` file:

```
using UnityEngine;
using System.Collections;

public class SimpleFSM : FSM {

    public enum FSMState {
        None, Patrol, Chase, Attack, Dead,
    }

    //Current state that the NPC is reaching
    public FSMState curState = FSMState.Patrol;

    //Speed of the tank
    private float curSpeed = 150.0f;

    //Tank Rotation Speed
    private float curRotSpeed = 2.0f;
```

```
//Bullet
public GameObject Bullet;

//Whether the NPC is destroyed or not
private bool bDead = false;
private int health = 100;

// We overwrite the deprecated built-in rigidbody
// variable.
new private Rigidbody rigidbody;

//Player Transform
protected Transform playerTransform;

//Next destination position of the NPC Tank
protected Vector3 destPos;

//List of points for patrolling
protected GameObject[] pointList;

//Bullet shooting rate
protected float shootRate = 3.0f;
protected float elapsedTime = 0.0f;
public float maxFireAimError = 0.001f;

// Status Radius
public float patrollingRadius = 100.0f;
public float attackRadius = 200.0f;
public float playerNearRadius = 300.0f;

//Tank Turret
public Transform turret;
public Transform bulletSpawnPoint;
```

Here, we declare a few variables. Our tank AI has four different states: **Patrol**, **Chase**, **Attack**, and **Dead**. We are implementing the FSM that we described as an example in *Chapter 1, Introduction to AI*:

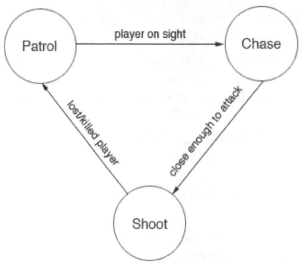

Figure 2.8 – The enemy tank AI's FSM

In our `Initialize` method, we set up our AI tank's properties with default values. Then, we store the positions of waypoints in our local variable. We get those waypoints from our scene using the `FindGameObjectsWithTag` method, trying to find those objects with the **WandarPoint** tag:

```
//Initialize the Finite state machine for the NPC tank
protected override void Initialize () {
    // Get the list of points
    pointList =
        GameObject.FindGameObjectsWithTag("WandarPoint");

    // Set Random destination point first
    FindNextPoint();

    // Get the target enemy (Player)
    GameObject objPlayer =
    GameObject.FindGameObjectWithTag("Player");
```

```
    // Get the rigidbody
    rigidbody = GetComponent<Rigidbody>();
    playerTransform = objPlayer.transform;
    if (!playerTransform) {
        print("Player doesn't exist. Please add one with
                Tag named 'Player'");
    }
}
```

The Update method that gets called every frame looks like the following:

```
protected override void FSMUpdate() {
    switch (curState) {
        case FSMState.Patrol:
            UpdatePatrolState();
            break;
        case FSMState.Chase:
            UpdateChaseState();
            break;
        case FSMState.Attack:
            UpdateAttackState();
            break;
        case FSMState.Dead:
            UpdateDeadState();
            break;
    }

    // Update the time
    elapsedTime += Time.deltaTime;

    // Go to dead state is no health left
    if (health <= 0) {
        curState = FSMState.Dead;
    }
}
```

We check the current state and then call the appropriate state method. Once the health object has a value of zero or less, we set the tank to the `Dead` state.

> **Debugging Private Variables**
>
> A public variable in the Inspector is not only useful because we can quickly experiment with different values but also because we can quickly look at a glance at their value when debugging. For this reason, you may even be tempted to make public (or expose to the Inspector) variables that should not be changed by the component's user. Don't worry – there is a solution: you can show the Inspector in **Debug** mode. In **Debug** mode, the Inspector also shows private fields. To enable Debug mode, click on the three dots at the top right and then click on **Debug**:

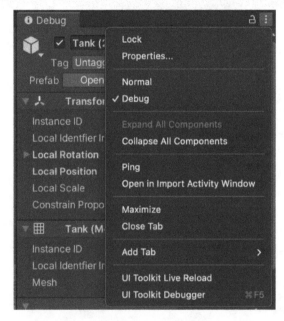

Figure 2.9 – Unity's Inspector in Debug mode

Now, let's see how to implement each state one by one.

The Patrol state

The **Patrol** state is the state in which the tank moves from waypoint to waypoint, looking for the player. The **Patrol** state's code is shown here:

```
protected void UpdatePatrolState() {
    if (Vector3.Distance(transform.position, destPos) <=
```

```
          patrollingRadius) {
      print("Reached to the destination point\n
              calculating the next point");
      FindNextPoint();
  } else if (Vector3.Distance(transform.position,
      playerTransform.position) <= playerNearRadius) {
      print("Switch to Chase Position");
      curState = FSMState.Chase;
  }


  // Rotate to the target point
  Quaternion targetRotation = Quaternion.LookRotation(
    destPos - transform.position);
  transform.rotation = Quaternion.Slerp(
    transform.rotation, targetRotation,
    Time.deltaTime * curRotSpeed);


  // Go Forward
  transform.Translate(Vector3.forward * Time.deltaTime *
                      curSpeed);
}


protected void FindNextPoint() {
    print("Finding next point");
    int rndIndex = Random.Range(0, pointList.Length);
    float rndRadius = 10.0f;
    Vector3 rndPosition = Vector3.zero;
    destPos = pointList[rndIndex].transform.position +
      rndPosition;


    // Check Range to decide the random point as the same
    // as before
    if (IsInCurrentRange(destPos)) {
        rndPosition = new Vector3(Random.Range(-rndRadius,
          rndRadius), 0.0f, Random.Range(-rndRadius,
          rndRadius));
```

```
                destPos = pointList[rndIndex].transform.position +
                    rndPosition;
        }
    }


protected bool IsInCurrentRange(Vector3 pos) {
    float xPos = Mathf.Abs(pos.x - transform.position.x);
    float zPos = Mathf.Abs(pos.z - transform.position.z);

    if (xPos <= 50 && zPos <= 50) return true;

    return false;
}
```

While our tank is in the **Patrol** state, we check whether it has reached the destination point (that is, if the tank is100 units or less from the destination waypoint). If so, it finds the next point to reach using the FindNextPoint method. This method simply chooses a random point from among the waypoints we defined before.

On the other hand, if the tank has not reached its destination point, it checks the distance to the player's tank. If the player's tank is in range (which, in this example, we choose to be 300 units), the AI switches to the **Chase** state. Finally, we use the remaining code in the UpdatePatrolState function to rotate the tank and move it toward the next waypoint.

The Chase state

In the **Chase** state, the tank actively tries to get near the player's tank. In simple terms, the destination point becomes the player's tank itself. The **Chase** state implementation code is shown here:

```
protected void UpdateChaseState() {
    // Set the target position as the player position
    destPos = playerTransform.position;

    // Check the distance with player tank When
    // the distance is near, transition to attack state
    float dist = Vector3.Distance(transform.position,
        playerTransform.position);
```

```
    if (dist <= attackRadius) {
        curState = FSMState.Attack;
    } else if (dist >= playerNearRadius {
        curState = FSMState.Patrol;
    }


    transform.Translate(Vector3.forward * Time.deltaTime *
                        curSpeed);
}
```

In this state, we first set the destination point as the player. Then, we continue checking the player's distance from the tank. If the player is close enough, the AI switches to the **Attack** state. On the other hand, if the player's tank manages to escape and goes too far, the AI goes back to the **Patrol** state.

The Attack state

The **Attack** state is precisely what you expect: the enemy tank aims and shoots at the player. The following code block is the implementation code for the **Attack** state:

```
protected void UpdateAttackState() {
    destPos = playerTransform.position;


    Vector3 frontVector = Vector3.forward;


    float dist = Vector3.Distance(transform.position,
        playerTransform.position);
    if (dist >= attackRadius && dist < playerNearRadius {
        Quaternion targetRotation =
            Quaternion. FromToRotation(destPos -
                                        transform.position);
        transform.rotation = Quaternion.Slerp(
            transform.rotation, targetRotation,
            Time.deltaTime * curRotSpeed);
        transform.Translate(Vector3.forward *
                            Time.deltaTime * curSpeed);


        curState = FSMState.Attack;
```

```
        } else if (dist >= playerNearRadius) {
            curState = FSMState.Patrol;
        }


        // Rotate the turret to the target point
        // The rotation is only around the vertical axis of the
        // tank.
        Quaternion targetRotation = Quaternion.FromToRotation(
            frontVector, destPos - transform.position);
        turret.rotation = Quaternion.Slerp(turret.rotation,
            turretRotation, Time.deltaTime * curRotSpeed);


        //Shoot the bullets
        if (Mathf.Abs(Quaternion.Dot(turretRotation,
            turret.rotation)) > 1.0f - maxFireAimError) {
            ShootBullet();
        }
    }


    private void ShootBullet() {
        if (elapsedTime >= shootRate) {
            Instantiate(Bullet, bulletSpawnPoint.position,
                    bulletSpawnPoint.rotation);
            elapsedTime = 0.0f;
        }
    }
```

In the first line, we still set the destination point to the player's position. After all, even when attacking, we need to keep a close distance from the player. Then, if the player tank is close enough, the AI tank rotates the turret object in the direction of the player tank and then starts shooting. Finally, if the player's tank goes out of range, the tank goes back to the **Patrol** state.

The Dead state

The **Dead** state is the final state. Once a tank is in the **Dead** state, it explodes and gets uninstantiated. The following is the code for the **Dead** state:

```
protected void UpdateDeadState() {
    // Show the dead animation with some physics effects
    if (!bDead) {
        bDead = true;
        Explode();
    }
}
```

As you can see, the code is straightforward – if the tank has reached the **Dead** state, we make it explode:

```
protected void Explode() {
    float rndX = Random.Range(10.0f, 30.0f);
    float rndZ = Random.Range(10.0f, 30.0f);
    for (int i = 0; i < 3; i++) {
        rigidbody.AddExplosionForce(10000.0f,
            transform.position - new Vector3(rndX,
            10.0f, rndZ), 40.0f, 10.0f);
        rigidbody.velocity = transform.TransformDirection(
            new Vector3(rndX, 20.0f, rndZ));
    }

    Destroy(gameObject, 1.5f);
}
```

Here's a small function that gives a nice explosion effect. We apply a random `ExplosionForce` function to the tank's `Rigidbody` component. If everything is correct, you should see the tank flying in the air in a random direction for the player's amusement.

Taking damage

To complete the demo, we need to add another small detail: we need the tanks to take damage when they get hit by a bullet. Every time a bullet enters the collision area of the tank, the health property's value decreases, according to the Bullet object's damage value:

```
void OnCollisionEnter(Collision collision) {
    // Reduce health
    if(collision.gameObject.tag == "Bullet") {
        health -=collision.gameObject.GetComponent
            <Bullet>().damage;
    }
}
```

You can open the SimpleFSM.scene file in Unity; you should see the AI tanks patrolling, chasing, and attacking the player. Our player's tank doesn't take damage from AI tanks yet, so it never gets destroyed. But the AI tanks have the health property and take damage from the player's bullets, so you'll see them explode once their health property reaches zero.

If your demo doesn't work, try playing with different values in the Inspector for the **SimpleFSM** components. After all, the values may change, depending on the scale of your project:

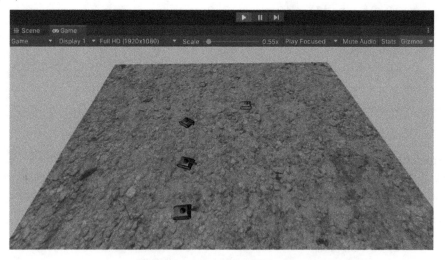

Figure 2.10 – The AI tanks in action

In this demo, we used a very simple FSM, but now it's time to step up the challenge and implement a complete FSM framework.

Using an FSM framework

The FSM framework we're going to use here is adapted from the **Deterministic Finite State Machine** framework, based on *Chapter 3.1* of *Game Programming Gems 1* by Eric Dybsend. We'll only be looking at the differences between this FSM and the one we made earlier. For this reason, it is important that you follow the example code found in the `Chapter02` folder of the book repository (`https://github.com/PacktPublishing/Unity-Artificial-Intelligence-Programming-Fifth-Edition`). In particular, we will look at the **AdvancedFSM** scene.

In this section, we will study how the framework works and how we can use this to implement our tank AI. `AdvancedFSM` and `FSMState` are the two main classes of our framework. So, let's take a look at them first.

The AdvancedFSM class

The `AdvancedFSM` class manages all the `FSMState` classes we've implemented and keeps them updated with the transitions and the current state. So, the first thing to do before using our framework is to declare the transitions and states that we plan to implement for our AI tanks.

Let's start by creating `AdvancedFSM.cs`:

```
using UnityEngine;
using System.Collections;
using System.Collections.Generic;

public enum Transition {
    None = 0, SawPlayer, ReachPlayer, LostPlayer, NoHealth,
}

public enum FSMStateID {
    None = 0, Patrolling, Chasing, Attacking, Dead,
}
```

Here, we define two enumerations, one for the set of states and one for the set of transitions. Then, we add a list object to store the `FSMState` objects and two local variables to store the current ID of the `FSMState` class and the current `FSMState` itself.

The `AddFSMState` and `DeleteState` methods add and delete the instances of the `FSMState` class in our list respectively. When the `PerformTransition` method gets called, it updates the `CurrentState` variable with the new state, according to the transition:

```
public class AdvancedFSM : FSM {
    private List<FSMState> fsmStates;
    private FSMStateID currentStateID;

    public FSMStateID CurrentStateID {
        get {
            return currentStateID;
        }
    }

    private FSMState currentState;

    public FSMState CurrentState {
        get {
            return currentState;
        }
    }
}
```

Now that the data part of the class is ready, we can proceed with the internal logic of the FSM framework.

The FSMState class

`FSMState` manages the transitions to other states. It has a dictionary object called map in which we store the key-value pairs of transitions and states. So, for example, the `SawPlayer` transition maps to the `Chasing` state, `LostPlayer` maps to the `Patrolling` state, and so on.

Let's create an `FSMState.cs` file:

```
using UnityEngine;
using System.Collections;
```

```
using System.Collections.Generic;

public abstract class FSMState {
    protected Dictionary<Transition, FSMStateID> map =
      new Dictionary<Transition, FSMStateID>();

    // Continue...
```

The `AddTransition` and `DeleteTransition` methods add and delete transitions from their state-transition dictionary map object. The `GetOutputState` method looks up from the `map` object and returns the state based on the input transition.

The `FSMState` class also declares two abstract methods that its child classes need to implement. They are as follows:

```
...
    public abstract void CheckTransitionRules(Transform
      player, Transform npc);
    public abstract void RunState(Transform player,
      Transform npc);
...
```

The `CheckTransitionRules` method has to check whether the state should carry out the transition to another state. Instead, the `RunState` method does the actual execution of the tasks for the `currentState` variable, such as moving toward a destination point and chasing or attacking the player. Both methods require transformed data from the player and the **Non Playable Character** (**NPC**) entity obtained using this class.

The state classes

Unlike the previous `SimpleFSM` example, we write the states for our tank AI in separate classes that inherit from the `FSMState` class, such as `AttackState`, `ChaseState`, `DeadState`, and `PatrolState`. All of them implement the `CheckTransitionRules` and `RunState` methods. Let's take a look at the `PatrolState` class as an example.

The PatrolState class

This class has three methods: a constructor, `CheckTransitionRules`, and `RunState`. Let's create the `PatrolState` class in the `PatrolState.cs` file:

```csharp
using UnityEngine;
using System.Collections;

public class PatrolState : FSMState {
    private Vector3 destPos;
    private Transform[] waypoints;
    private float curRotSpeed = 1.0f;
    private float curSpeed = 100.0f;
    private float playerNearRadius;
    private float patrollRadius;

    public PatrolState(Transform[] wp, float
      playerNearRadius, float patrollRadius) {
        waypoints = wp;
        stateID = FSMStateID.Patrolling;
        this.playerNearRadius = playerNearRadius;
        this.patrollRadius = patrollRadius;
    }

    public override void CheckTransitionRules(
      Transform player, Transform npc) {
        // Check the distance with player tank
        // When the distance is near, transition to chase
        // state
        if (Vector3.Distance(npc.position, player.position)
            <= playerNearRadius) {
            Debug.Log("Switch to Chase State");
            NPCTankController npcTankController =
                npc.GetComponent<NPCTankController>();
            if (npcTankController != null) {
```

```
                    npcTankController.SetTransition(
                    Transition.SawPlayer);
            } else {
                    Debug.LogError("NPCTankController not found
                                in NPC");
            }
        }
    }

    public override void RunState(Transform player,
        Transform npc) {
        // Find another random patrol point if the current
        // point is reached

        if (Vector3.Distance(npc.position, destPos) <=
            patrollRadius) {
            Debug.Log("Reached to the destination point\n
                        calculating the next point");
            FindNextPoint();
        }

        // Rotate to the target point
        Quaternion targetRotation =
            Quaternion.FromToRotation(Vector3.forward,
            destPos - npc.position);
        npc.rotation = Quaternion.Slerp(npc.rotation,
            targetRotation, Time.deltaTime * curRotSpeed);

        // Go Forward
        npc.Translate(Vector3.forward * Time.deltaTime *
                    curSpeed);
    }
}
```

The `constructor` method takes the `waypoints` array, stores them in a local array, and then initializes properties such as movement and rotation speed. The `Reason` method checks the distance between itself (the AI tank) and the player tank. If the player tank is in range, it sets the transition ID to the `SawPlayer` transition using the `SetTransition` method of the `NPCTankController` class, which looks as follows:

```
public void SetTransition(Transition t) {
    PerformTransition(t);
}
```

The preceding function is just a wrapper method that calls the `PerformTransition` method of the `AdvanceFSM` class. In turn, that method updates the `CurrentState` variable with the one responsible for this transition, using the `Transition` object and the state-transition dictionary map object from the `FSMState` class. The `Act` method updates the AI tank's destination point, rotates the tank in that direction, and moves it forward.

Other state classes also follow this template with different reasoning and acting procedures. We've already seen them in our previous simple FSM examples, and therefore, we won't describe them again here. See whether you can figure out how to set up these classes on your own. If you get stuck, the assets that come with this book contain the code for you to look at.

The NPCTankController class

For the tank AI, we set up the states for our NPC by using the `NPCTankController` class. This class inherits from `AdvanceFSM`:

```
private void ConstructFSM() {
    PatrolState patrol = new PatrolState(waypoints,
        playerNearRadius, patrollingRadius);
    patrol.AddTransition(Transition.SawPlayer,
                    FSMStateID.Chasing);
    patrol.AddTransition(Transition.NoHealth,
                    FSMStateID.Dead);

    ChaseState chase = new ChaseState(waypoints);
    chase.AddTransition(Transition.LostPlayer,
                    FSMStateID.Patrolling);
```

```
    chase.AddTransition(Transition.ReachPlayer,
                    FSMStateID.Attacking);
    chase.AddTransition(Transition.NoHealth,
                    FSMStateID.Dead);


    AttackState attack = new AttackState(waypoints);
    attack.AddTransition(Transition.LostPlayer,
                    FSMStateID.Patrolling);
    attack.AddTransition(Transition.SawPlayer,
                    FSMStateID.Chasing);
    attack.AddTransition(Transition.NoHealth,
                    FSMStateID.Dead);


    DeadState dead = new DeadState();
    dead.AddTransition(Transition.NoHealth,
                    FSMStateID.Dead);
    AddFSMState(patrol);
    AddFSMState(chase);
    AddFSMState(attack);
    AddFSMState(dead);
}
```

Here's the beauty of using our FSM framework: since the states are self-managed within their respective classes, our NPCTankController class only needs to call the Reason and Act methods of the currently active state.

This fact eliminates the need to write a long list of the if/else and switch statements. Instead, our states are now nicely packaged in classes of their own, which makes the code more manageable, as the number of states and transitions between them grows more and more in larger projects:

```
protected override void FSMFixedUpdate() {
    CurrentState.Reason(playerTransform, transform);
    CurrentState.Act(playerTransform, transform);
}
```

The main steps to use this framework can be summarized as follows:

1. Declare the transitions and states in the `AdvanceFSM` class.

2. Write the state classes inherited from the `FSMState` class, and then implement the `Reason` and `Act` methods.

3. Write the custom NPC AI class inherited from `AdvanceFSM`.

4. Create states from the state classes, and then add transition and state pairs using the `AddTransition` method of the `FSMState` class.

5. Add those states into the state list of the `AdvanceFSM` class, using the `AddFSMState` method.

6. Call the `CurrentState` variable's `Reason` and `Act` methods in the game update cycle.

You can play around with the `AdvancedFSM` scene in Unity. It'll run the same way as our previous `SimpleFSM` example, but the code is now more organized and manageable.

Summary

In this chapter, we learned how to implement state machines in Unity3D based on a simple tank game. We first looked at how to implement FSM by using `switch` statements. Then, we studied how to use a framework to make AI implementation easier to manage and extend.

In the next chapter, we will look at randomness and probability and see how we can use them to make the outcome of our games more unpredictable.

3
Randomness and Probability

In this chapter, we will look at how we can apply the concepts of probability and randomness to game AI. Because we will talk more about the use of randomness in game AI and less about Unity3D, we can apply the concepts of this chapter to any game development middleware or technology framework. We'll be using Mono C# in Unity3D for the demos, but we won't address much on the specific features of the Unity3D engine and the editor itself.

Game developers use probability to add a little uncertainty to the behaviors of AI characters and the wider game world. Randomness makes artificial intelligence look more realistic and natural, and it is the perfect "spice" for all those cases in which we do not need *intentional* predictability.

In this chapter, we will look at the following topics:

- Introducing randomness in Unity
- Learning the basics of probability
- Exploring more examples of probability in games
- Creating a slot machine

Technical requirements

For this chapter, you just need Unity3D 2022. You can find the example project described in this chapter in the `Chapter 3` folder in the book repository: `https://github.com/PacktPublishing/Unity-Artificial-Intelligence-Programming-Fifth-Edition/tree/main/Chapter03`.

Introducing randomness in Unity

Game designers and developers use randomness in game AI to make a game and its characters more realistic by altering the outcomes of characters' decisions.

Let's take an example of a typical soccer game. One of the rules of a soccer game is to award a direct free kick to a team if one opposing team player commits a foul while trying to retake control of the ball. However, instead of giving a free kick whenever that foul happens, the game developer can apply a probability to reward only 98% of all the fouls with a direct free kick.

After all, in reality, referees make mistakes sometimes. As a result of this simple change, the player usually gets a direct free kick as expected. Still, when that remaining two percent happens, the game provides more emotional feedback to both teams (assuming that you are playing against another human, one player will be happy while the other will complain with the virtual referee).

Of course, randomness is not always a desirable perk of AI. As we anticipated in the introduction, some level of predictability allows players to learn the AI patterns, and understanding the AI patterns is often the main component of gameplay. For example, in a stealth game, learning the enemy guards' paths is necessary to allow the player to find a sneaking route. Or imagine you need to design a boss for a game such as *Dark Souls*.

Learning the big boss attack patterns is the player's primary weapon and the only proper way to achieve mastery for boss fights. As always, you have to follow the polar star of game design: do only what it is fun for the player. If adding randomness adds only frustration for the players, then you should remove it without exceptions.

However, in some cases, a bit of randomness is useful, and for some games, such as gambling minigames, it is a necessary prerequisite. In those cases, how can a computer produce random values? And more importantly, how can we use random numbers in Unity?

Randomness in computer science

Computers are deterministic machines: by design, if we give a computer the same input multiple times, in the form of program code and data, it always returns the same output. Therefore, how can we have a program return unpredictable and random output?

If we need genuinely random numbers, then we need to take this randomness from somewhere else. That's why many advanced applications try to combine different external sources of randomness into a random value: they may look at the movement of the mouse during a specific interval, to the noise of the internet connection, or even ask the user to smash the keyboard randomly, and so on. There is even dedicated hardware for random number generation!

Fortunately, in games, we do not need such genuinely random numbers, and we can use simpler algorithms that can generate sequences that look like a sequence of random numbers. Such algorithms are called **Pseudorandom Number Generators** (**PRNGs**). Using an initial seed, they can generate, in a deterministic way, a sequence of numbers that statistically approximate the properties of a sequence of truly random numbers. The catch is that if we start from the same seed, we always get the same sequence of numbers.

For this reason, we usually initialize the seed value from something that we imagine is always different every time the user opens the application, such as, for instance, the elapsed time in milliseconds since the computer started running, or the number of milliseconds since 1970 (the *Unix timestamp*). Note, however, that having the possibility to obtain the same random sequence every time is truly beneficial when debugging!

Finally, note that some PRNGs are more random than others. If we were creating an encryption program, we would want to look into less predictable PRNGs, called **Cryptographically Secure Pseudorandom Number Generators** (**CSPRNGs**). Fortunately, for games, the simple **Random Number Generation** (**RNG**) that comes with Unity is good enough.

The Unity Random class

The Unity3D script has a `Random` class to generate random data. You can set the generator seed using the `InitState(int seed)` function. Usually, we wouldn't want to repeatedly seed the same value, as this generates the same predictable sequence of random numbers at each execution.

However, there are some cases in which we want to give the user control over the seed – for instance, when we test the game or want the players to generate a procedural map/level with a specific seed. Then, you can read the `Random.value` property to get a random number between 0.0 and 1.0. This generator is inclusive, and therefore, this property can return both 0.0 and 1.0.

For example, in the following snippet, we generate a random color by choosing a random value between 0 and 1 for the red, green, and blue components:

```
Color randomColor = new Color(Random.value, Random.value,
Random.value);
```

Another class method that can be quite handy is the `Range` method:

```
static function Range (min : float, max : float) : float
```

We can use the `Range` method to generate a random number from a range. When given an integer value, it returns a random integer number between `min` (inclusive) and `max` (exclusive). Therefore, if we set `min` to 1 and `max` to 4, we can get 1, 2, or 3, but never 4. Instead, if we use the `Range` function for float values, both `min` and `max` are inclusive, meaning we can get 1.0, or 4.0, or all the floats in between. Take note whenever a parameter is exclusive or inclusive because it is a common source of bugs (and confusion) when using the Unity `Random` class.

A simple random dice game

Let's set up a straightforward dice game in a new scene where we need to guess the output of a six-sided dice (simulated by generating a random integer between one and six). The player wins if the input value matches the dice result generated randomly, as shown in the following `DiceGame.cs` file:

```
using UnityEngine;
using TMPro;
using UnityEngine.UI;

public class DiceGame : MonoBehaviour {
    public string inputValue = "1";

    public TMP_Text outputText;
    public TMP_InputField inputField;
    public Button button;

    int throwDice() {
        Debug.Log("Throwing dice...");
```

```
        Debug.Log("Finding random between 1 to 6...");
        int diceResult = Random.Range(1,7);

        Debug.Log($"Result: {diceResult}");

        return diceResult;
    }


    public void processGame() {
        inputValue = inputField.text;
        try {
            int inputInteger = int.Parse(inputValue);
            int totalSix = 0;
            for (var i = 0; i < 10; i++) {
                var diceResult = throwDice();
                if (diceResult == 6) { totalSix++; }

                if (diceResult == inputInteger) {
                    outputText.text = $"DICE RESULT:
                      {diceResult} \r\nYOU WIN!";
                } else {
                    outputText.text = $"DICE RESULT:
                      {diceResult} \r\nYOU LOSE!";
                }
            }
            Debug.Log($"Total of six: {totalSix}");
        } catch {
            outputText.text = "Input is not a number!";
            Debug.LogError("Input is not a number!");
        }
    }
}
```

In the previous code, we saw the `DiceGame` class that implements the whole game. However, we still need to set up the scene with the appropriate UI object to accept the player's inputs and display the results:

1. First, we need to create `guiText` to show the result. Click on **Game Object | UI | Text - TextMeshPro**. This will add `New Text` text to the game scene.

2. Center it at the top of the canvas.

3. Then, in the same way, create a button by selecting **Game Object | UI | Button – TextMeshPro** and an input field by selecting **Game Object | UI | Input Field – TextMeshPro**.

4. Arrange them vertically on the screen.

5. Create an empty game object and call it `DiceGame`. At this point, you should have something similar to *Figure 3.1*:

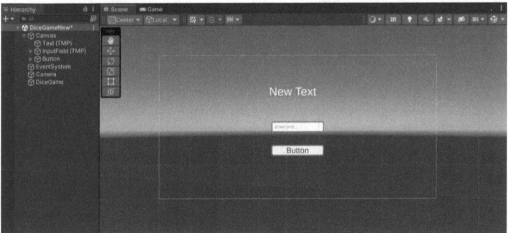

Figure 3.1 – Our simple Unity interface

6. Select the text inside the button and replace `Button` with `Play!` in the **TextMeshPro** component.

7. Select the New Text text and replace it with Result: in the **TextMeshPro** component:

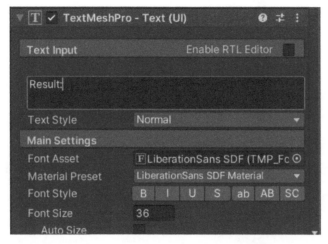

Figure 3.2 – The TextMeshPro component

8. Now, attach the DiceGame component to the DiceGame object, and connect into the DiceGame component the tree UI elements that we created before:

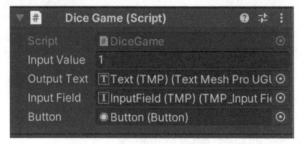

Figure 3.3 – The DiceGame component

9. Finally, select `Button` and look for the `onClick()` section in the `Button` component. Drag and drop the `DiceGame` object into the field with `None` `(GameObject)` and select **DiceGame | processGame ()** from the drop-down menu. This will connect the `processGame` function to the click event for the button:

Figure 3.4 – The On Click event configuration

At this point, the game should be ready. Click Unity's play button and give it a go.

To successfully manage random numbers, we need to have a basic understanding of the laws of probability. So, that's what we are going to learn in the next section.

Learning the basics of probability

There are many ways to define probability. The most intuitive definition of probability is called **frequentism**. According to frequentism, the probability of an event is the frequency with which the event occurs when we repeat the observation an infinite amount of times. In other words, if we throw a die 100 times, we expect to see a six, on average, 1/6th of the times, and we should get closer and closer to 1/6th with 1,000, 10,000, and 1 million throws.

We can write the probability of event A occurring as *P(A)*. To calculate *P(A)*, we need to know all the possible outcomes (*N*) for the observation and the total number of times in which the desired event occurs (*n*).

We can calculate the probability of event *A* as follows:

$$P(A) = \frac{n}{N}$$

If *P(A)* is the probability of event *A* happening, then the probability of event *A* not happening is equal to the following:

$$\bar{P} = 1 - P(A)$$

The probability must be a real number between zero and one. Having a probability of zero means that there's no chance of the desired event happening; on the other hand, having a probability of one means that the event will occur for sure. As a consequence, the following must equal to one:

$$P(A) + \bar{P}(A) = 1$$

However, not all events are alike. One of the most critical concepts in probability calculus is the concept of *independent and non-independent events*. That's the topic of the next section.

Independent and correlated events

Another important concept in probability is whether the chance of a particular event occurring depends on any other event somehow. For example, consider throwing a six-sided die twice and getting a double six. Each die throw can be viewed as an independent event. Each time you throw a die, the probability of each side turning up is one in six, and the outcome of the second die roll does not change depending on the result of the first roll. On the other hand, in drawing two aces from the same deck, each draw is not independent of the others. If you drew an ace in the first event, the probability of getting another ace the second time is different because there is now one less ace in the deck (and one less card in the deck).

The independence of events is crucial because it significantly simplifies some calculations. For instance, imagine that we want to know the probability of either event A or event B happening. If A and B are two independent events, then we can add the probabilities of A and B:

$$P(A \text{ or } B) = P(A) + P(B)$$

In the same way, if we want to know the probability that both A and B occur, then we can multiply the individual probabilities together:

$$P(A \text{ and } B) = P(A) \cdot P(B)$$

For instance, if we want to know the probability of getting two sixes by throwing two dice, we can multiply 1/6 by 1/6 to get the correct probability: 1/36.

Conditional probability

Now, let's consider another example. We are still throwing two dice, but this time, we are interested in the probability that the sum of the numbers showing up on two dice is equal to two. Since there's only one way to get this sum, one plus one, the probability is the same as getting the same number on both dice. In that case, it would still be 1/36.

But how about getting the sum of the numbers that show up on the two dice to seven? As you can see, there are a total of six possible ways of getting a total of seven, outlined in the following table:

Dice 1	Dice 2
1	6
2	5
3	4
4	3
5	2
6	1

Figure 3.5 – The possible outcomes of two dice

In this case, we need to use the general probability formula. From the preceding table, we can see that we have six outcomes that give us a total sum of seven. Because we know that there are 36 total possible outcomes for 2 dice, we can quickly compute the final probability as 6/36 or, simplifying, one-sixth (16.7%).

Loaded dice

Now, let's assume that we haven't been all too honest, and our dice are loaded so that the side of the number six has a double chance of landing facing upward. Since we doubled the chance of getting six, we need to double the probability of getting six – let's say, up to roughly one-third (0.34) – and as a consequence, the rest is equally spread over the remaining five sides (0.132 each).

We can implement a loaded dice algorithm this way: first, we generate a random value between 1 and 100. Then, we check whether the random value falls between 1 and 35. If so, our algorithm returns six; otherwise, we get a random dice value between one and five (since these values have the same probability).

For this, we create a new class called `DiceGameLoaded`. The game is identical to `DiceGame` but with an important difference: the `throwDice` function is changed, as follows:

```
int throwDice() {
    Debug.Log("Throwing dice...");

    int randomProbability = Random.Range(0, 100);
    int diceResult = 0;
    if (randomProbability < 35) {
        diceResult = 6;
    } else {
        diceResult = Random.Range(1, 5);
    }

    Debug.Log("Result: " + diceResult);

    return diceResult;
}
```

To try this new version of the game, swap the `DiceGame` component with the `DiceGame` component in the `DiceGame` object and rebind the `onClick` button event as we did before. If we test our new loaded dice algorithm by throwing the dice multiple times, you'll notice that the 6 value yields more than usual.

As you can see, the code is very similar to the non-loaded dice. However, this time, we are throwing an unfair dice that returns six much more than it should: we first select a random number between 0 and 100; if the number is less than 35, we return 6. Otherwise, we choose a random number between 1 and 5. Therefore, we get a 6 35% of the time and every other number roughly 15% of the time (we divide the remaining 75% by 5).

Remember that, in games, it's not cheating if the goal is to give the player a more exciting and fun experience!

Exploring more examples of probability in games

In this section, we will explore some of the most common applications of probability and randomness in video games.

Character personalities

Probability and randomness are not only about dice. We can also use a probability distribution to specify an in-game character's specialties. For example, let's pretend we designed a game proposal for a population management game for the local government. We need to address and simulate issues such as taxation versus global talent attraction, and immigration versus social cohesion. We have three types of characters in our proposal – namely, workers, scientists, and professionals. Their efficiencies in performing their particular tasks are defined in the following table:

Characters	Construction	Research and Development	Corporate jobs
Worker	95	2	3
Scientist	5	85	10
Professional	10	10	80

Figure 3.6 – The efficiency of every character in performing each task

Let's take a look at how we can implement this scenario. Let's say the player needs to build new houses to accommodate the increased population. A house construction would require 1,000 units of workload to finish. We use the earlier value as the workload that can be done per second per unit type for a particular task.

So, if you're building a house with one worker, it'll only take about 10 seconds to finish the construction (1000/95), whereas it'll take more than 3 minutes if you are trying to build with the scientists (1000/5 = 200 seconds). The same is true for other tasks, such as research and development and corporate jobs. Of course, these factors can be adjusted or enhanced later as the game progresses, making some entry-level tasks simpler and taking less time.

Then, we introduce special items that the particular unit type can discover. We don't want to give out these items every time a particular unit has done its tasks. Instead, we want to reward the player as a surprise. So, we associate the probability of finding such items according to the unit type, as described in the following table:

Special items	Worker	Scientist	Professional
Raw materials	0.3	0.1	0.0
New tech	0.0	0.3	0.0
Bonus	0.1	0.2	0.4

Figure 3.7 – The probability of finding specific objects for each unit type

The preceding table shows a 30% chance of a worker finding some raw materials and a 10% chance of earning bonus income whenever they have built a factory or a house. This allows the players to anticipate possible upcoming rewards once they've done some tasks and make the game more fun because they do not know the event's outcome.

Perceived randomness

One critical aspect of randomness is that humans are terrible at understanding true randomness. Instead, when us humans talk about *random results*, we think of *equally distributed results*. For example, imagine a **Massive Online Battle Arena** (**MOBA**) game such as *League of Legends*. Imagine that we have a hero with an ability that does colossal damage but only hits 50% of the time. The player starts a game with such a hero, but the hero misses that ability five times in a row due to bad luck. Put yourself in the shoes of that player – you would think that the computer is cheating or that there is something wrong, right?

However, getting 5 consecutive misses has a probability of 1 over 32. That is about 3.1%, more than getting three of a kind in a five-card deal of poker (which is about 2.1%) – unlikely but possible. If our game uses a perfectly random number generator, we may get this scenario relatively often.

Let's put it another way. Given a sequence of misses (*M*) and hits (*H*), which sequence do you find more *random* between *HHHHHMMM* and *HMHMHHMH*? I bet the second one, where we interleave misses and hits. It feels more random than the first one (where hits and misses are nicely grouped in strikes), even if they have the exact same chance of occurring naturally.

The point is that, sometimes, for the sake of player engagements, games need to tweak their randomness to get something that feels more random than true randomness. Video games do that in several ways. The most common one is keeping track of the number of occurrences of a value that should be perceived as random.

So, for instance, we may keep track of the number of hits and misses of our hero's ability, and when we see that the ratio between the two get too far away from the theoretical one of 50% – for example, when we have 75% misses (or hits) – we rebalance the ratio by forcing a hit (or vice versa).

FSM with probability

In *Chapter 2, Finite State Machines*, we saw how to implement an FSM using simple switch statements or the FSM framework. We based the decision on choosing which state to execute purely on a given condition's true or false value. Let's go back for a moment to the FSM of our AI-controlled tank entity:

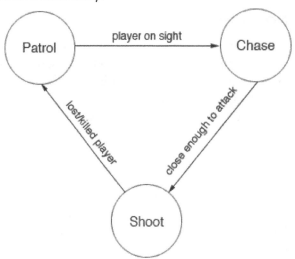

Figure 3.8 – The tank AI FSM

For the sake of the example, we can give our tank entities some options to choose from instead of doing the same thing whenever it meets a specific condition. For example, in our earlier FSM, our AI tank would always chase the player tank once the player was in its line of sight. Instead, we can split the **player on sight** transaction and connect it to an additional new state, **Flee**. How can the AI decide which state to move to? Randomly, of course:

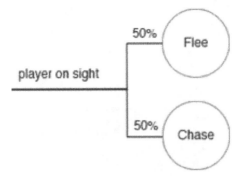

Figure 3.9 – FSM using probability

As shown in the preceding diagram, instead of chasing every time, now, when the AI tank spots the player, there's a 50% chance that it'll flee the scene (maybe to report the attack to the headquarters or something else). We can implement this mechanism the same way we did with our previous dice example. First, we must randomly get a value between 1 and 100 and see whether the value lies between 1 and 50, or 51 and 100. If it's the former, the tank will flee; otherwise, it will chase the player.

Another way to implement a random selection is by using the **roulette wheel selection algorithm**. This algorithm is advantageous when we do not have exact probabilities or know all the possible options at compile time (for instance, because we load the FSM rules from a file).

As the name suggests, the idea is to imagine a roulette wheel with one sector for each event. However, the more probable an event is, the larger the sector is. Then, we mathematically spin the wheel and choose the event corresponding to the sector where we ended up:

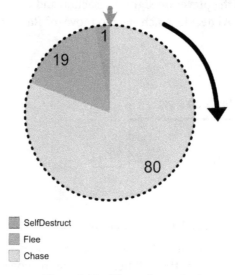

SelfDestruct

Flee

Chase

Figure 3.10 – The roulette wheel

In our example, we have three states: **Chase**, **Flee**, and **SelfDestruct**. We assign a weight to each state, representing how probable they are with respect to each other. For instance, in the figure, you can see that I set **Chase** with weight **80**, **Flee** with weight **19**, and **SelfDestruct** with weight **1**. Note that weights do not need to sum to 1 like probabilities, nor 100, nor anything in particular.

In this case, however, I made them add to 100 because it is easier to translate weights into probabilities: we can imagine **Chase** happening 80% of the time, **Flee** 19% of the time, and in 1% of the cases, the tank self-destructing. However, in general, you can imagine the weight of event X as the number of balls with X written on them and put inside a lottery box.

Let's see the result in the FSM.cs file:

```
using UnityEngine;
using System.Collections;
using System;


using System.Linq;


public class FSM : MonoBehaviour {

```

```
[Serializable]
public enum FSMState {
    Chase,
    Flee,
    SelfDestruct,
}


[Serializable]
public struct FSMProbability {
    public FSMState state;
    public int weight;
}


public FSMProbability[] states;


FSMState selectState() {
    // Sum the weights of every state.
    var weightSum = states.Sum(state => state.weight);
    var randomNumber = UnityEngine.Random.Range(0,
      weightSum);
    var i = 0;
    while (randomNumber >= 0) {
        var state = states[i];
        randomNumber -= state.weight;
        if (randomNumber <= 0) {
            return state.state;
        }
        i++;
    }
    // It is not possible to reach this point!
    throw new Exception("Something is wrong in the
      selectState algorithm!");
}


// Update is called once per frame
void Update () {
```

```
        if (Input.GetKeyDown(KeyCode.Space))
        {
            FSMState randomState = selectState();
            Debug.Log(randomState.ToString());
        }
    }
}
```

The mechanism is straightforward. First, we sum all the weights to know the size of the imaginary wheel. Then, we pick a number between 0 and this sum. Finally, we subtract from this number the weights of each state (starting from the first one) until the number gets negative. Then, as you can see in the `Update()` method, every time we press the *Spacebar*, the algorithm chooses one random item from our `states` array.

Dynamically adapting AI skills

We can also use probability to specify the intelligence levels of AI characters or the global game settings, affecting, in turn, a game's overall difficulty level to keep it challenging and exciting for the players. As described in the book *The Art of Game Design* by Jesse Schell, players only continue to play a game if the game keeps them in the flow channel (a concept adapted to games from the psychological works on flow state of Mihály Csíkszentmihályi):

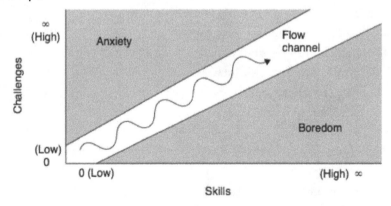

Figure 3.11 – The player's flow channel

If we present too tricky challenges to the players before they have the necessary skills, they will feel anxious and disappointed. On the other hand, once they've mastered the game, they will get bored if we keep it at the same pace. The area in which the players remain engaged for a long time is between these two hard and easy extremes, which the original author referred to as the flow channel. To keep the players in the flow channel, the game designers need to feed challenges and missions that match the increasing skills that the players acquire over time. However, it is not easy to find a value that works for all players, since the pace of learning and expectations can differ from individual to individual.

One way to tackle this problem is to collect the player's attempts and results during the gameplay sessions and to adjust the difficulty of the opponent's AI accordingly. So, how can we change the AI's difficulty – for instance, by making the AI more aggressive, increasing the probability of landing a perfect shot, or decreasing the probability of erratic behavior?

Creating a slot machine

In this demo, we will design and implement a slot machine game with 10 symbols and 3 reels. To make it simple, we'll use the numbers from zero to nine as our symbols. Many slot machines use fruit and other simple shapes, such as bells, stars, and letters. Some other slot machines use a specific theme based on popular movies or TV franchises. Since there are 10 symbols and 3 reels, that's a total of 1,000 (10^3) possible combinations.

A random slot machine

This random slot machine demo is similar to our previous dice example. This time, we are going to generate three random numbers for three reels. The only payout will be when we get three of the same symbols on the pay line. To make it simpler, we'll only have one line to play against in this demo. If the player wins, the game will return 500 times the bet amount.

We'll set up our scene with all our UI elements: three texts for the reels, another text element for the **YOU WIN** or **YOU LOSE** text (the betResult object), one text element for the player's credits (Credits), an input field for the bet (InputField), and a button to pull the lever (Button):

Figure 3.12 – Our GUI text objects

This is how our new script looks, as shown in the following SlotMachine.cs file:

```
using UnityEngine;
using UnityEngine.UI;

public class SlotMachine : MonoBehaviour {
    public float spinDuration = 2.0f;
    public int numberOfSym = 10;

    public Text firstReel;
    public Text secondReel;
    public Text thirdReel;
    public Text betResult;

    public Text totalCredits;
    public InputField inputBet;
    private bool startSpin = false;

    private bool firstReelSpinned = false;
    private bool secondReelSpinned = false;
    private bool thirdReelSpinned = false;
    private int betAmount;
    private int credits = 1000;
```

```
    private int firstReelResult = 0;
    private int secondReelResult = 0;
    private int thirdReelResult = 0;
    private float elapsedTime = 0.0f;
```

First, we start by listing all the class attributes we need. Again, note that it is a good programming practice to avoid public fields unless strictly necessary. Therefore, you should use the [SerializeField] attribute instead. Here, however, we will use the public attribute to avoid making the code listing too long.

Now, let's continue by adding three new functions: Spin, which starts the spinning of the slot machine; OnGui, which we will use to update the user interface; and checkBet, a function that checks the result of the spin and informs the players if they win or lose:

```
public void Spin() {
    if (betAmount > 0) {
        startSpin = true;
    } else {
        betResult.text = "Insert a valid bet!";
    }
}


private void OnGUI() {
    try {
        betAmount = int.Parse(inputBet.text);
    } catch {
        betAmount = 0;
    }
    totalCredits.text = credits.ToString();
}


void checkBet() {
    if (firstReelResult == secondReelResult &&
        secondReelResult == thirdReelResult) {
        betResult.text =
            "YOU WIN!"; credits += 500*betAmount;
    } else {
        betResult.text = "YOU LOSE!"; credits -= betAmount;
```

```
        }
    }
```

Next, we implement the main loop of the script. In the FixedUpdate function, we run the slot machine by spinning each reel in turn. In the beginning, firstReelSpinned, secondReelSpinned, and thirdReelSpinned are all false. Therefore, we enter in the first if block. Here, we set the reel to a random value, and we end the function. We repeat that until a certain amount of time has passed.

After that, we set the reel to the final value, and we set firstReelSpinned to true. Then, the function will move to the second reel, where we repeat these steps. Finally, after the third reel is finally set to its final value, we check the results with checkBet:

```
void FixedUpdate () {
    if (startSpin) {
        elapsedTime += Time.deltaTime;
        int randomSpinResult =
          Random.Range(0, numberOfSym);
        if (!firstReelSpinned) {
            firstReel.text = randomSpinResult.ToString();
            if (elapsedTime >= spinDuration) {
                firstReelResult = randomSpinResult;
                firstReelSpinned = true;
                elapsedTime = 0;
            }
        } else if (!secondReelSpinned) {
            secondReel.text = randomSpinResult.ToString();
            if (elapsedTime >= spinDuration) {
                secondReelResult = randomSpinResult;
                secondReelSpinned = true;
                elapsedTime = 0;
            }
        } else if (!thirdReelSpinned) {
```

```
            thirdReel.text = randomSpinResult.ToString();
        if (elapsedTime >= spinDuration) {
            thirdReelResult = randomSpinResult;
            startSpin = false;
            elapsedTime = 0;
            firstReelSpinned = false;
            secondReelSpinned = false;
            checkBet();
        }
    }
  }
}
```

Attach the script to an empty `GameController` object and then fill in the referenced object in the Inspector. Then, we need to connect `Button` to the `Spin()` method. To do that, select `Button` and fill the **On Click ()** event handler in the Inspector, as shown in the following screenshot:

Figure 3.13 – The On Click() event handler

When we click the button, we set the `startSpin` flag to `true`. Once spinning, in the `FixedUpdate()` method, we generate a random value for each reel. Finally, once we've got the value for the third reel, we reset the `startSpin` flag to `false`. While we are getting the random value for each reel, we also track how much time has elapsed since the player pulled the lever.

Usually, each reel would take 3 to 5 seconds before landing the result in real-world slot machines. Hence, we also take some time, as specified in `spinDuration`, before showing the final random value. If you play the scene and click on the **Pull Lever** button, you should see the final result, as shown in the following screenshot:

Figure 3.14 – Our random slot game in action

Since your chance of winning is 1 out of 100, it quickly becomes tedious, as you lose several times consecutively. However, if you've ever played a slot machine, this is not how it works, or at least not anymore. Usually, you can have several wins during your play. Even though these small wins don't recoup your principal bet (and in the long run, most players go broke), the slot machines still occasionally render winning graphics and exciting sounds, which researchers refer to as losses disguised as wins.

So, instead of just one single way to win the jackpot, we want to modify the rules a bit so that the slot machine pays out smaller returns during the play session.

Weighted probability

Real slot machines have something called a **Paytable and Reel Strips** (**PARS**) sheet, which is the complete design document of the machine. The PARS sheet is used to specify the payout percentage, the winning patterns, their payouts, and so on.

The number of payout prizes and the frequencies of such wins must be carefully selected so that the house (the slot machine) always wins in the long run while making sure to return something to the players from time to time to make the machine attractive to play. This is known as payback percentage or **Return to Player** (**RTP**). For example, a slot machine with a 90% RTP means that, over time, the machine returns an average of 90% of all bets to the players.

In this demo, we will not focus on choosing the house's optimal value to yield specific wins over time, nor maintaining a particular payback percentage. Instead, we will demonstrate how to weight probability for specific symbols showing up more times than usual. So, let's say we want to make the 0 symbols appear 20% more than usual on the first and third reel and return half of the bet as a payout.

In other words, a player only loses half of their bet if they got zero symbols on the first and third reels, essentially disguising a loss as a small win. Currently, the zero symbols have a probability of 1/10th (0.1), or a 10% probability. We'll change this now to a 30% chance of zero landing on the first and third reels, as shown in the following SlotMachineWeighted.cs file (remember to switch to the SlotMachineWeighted component in the example code!):

```
using UnityEngine;
using System.Collections;
using UnityEngine.UI;

public class SlotMachineWeighted : MonoBehaviour {
    public float spinDuration = 2.0f;
    // Number of symbols on the slot machine reels
    public int numberOfSym = 10;

    public Text firstReel;
    public Text secondReel;
    public Text thirdReel;
    public Text betResult;

    public Text totalCredits;
    public InputField inputBet;

    private bool startSpin = false;
    private bool firstReelSpinned = false;
    private bool secondReelSpinned = false;
    private bool thirdReelSpinned = false;
    private int betAmount = 100;
    private int credits = 1000;

    [Serializable]
```

```
public struct WeightedProbability {
    public int number;
    public int weight;
}
private List<WeightedProbability> weightedReelPoll =
    new List<WeightedProbability>();
private int zeroProbability = 30;
private int firstReelResult = 0;
private int secondReelResult = 0;
private int thirdReelResult = 0;
private float elapsedTime = 0.0f;
```

New variable declarations are added, such as `zeroProbability`, to specify the probability percentage of the zero symbols landing on the first and third reels. For example, if `zeroProbability` is 30, the third reel will show 0 30% of the time. The `weightedReelPoll` array list is used to fill the weighted symbols, as we did in our earlier FSM example.

Then, we initialize this list in the `Start()` method, as shown in the following code:

```
void Start () {
    weightedReelPoll.Add(new WeightedProbability {
        number = 0,
        weight = zeroProbability
    });

    int remainingValuesProb = (100 - zeroProbability)/9;

    for (int i = 1; i < 10; i++) {
        weightedReelPoll.Add(new WeightedProbability {
        number = i,
        weight = remainingValuesProb
    });
}}
```

In practice, we set the value for 0 to 30, and we split the remaining 70 percentage points between the remaining 9 numbers.

We are also writing a revised and improved `checkBet()` method. Instead of just one jackpot win option, we are now considering five conditions of jackpot: loss disguised as a win, a near miss, any two symbols matched on the first and third row, and of course, the `lose` condition:

```
void checkBet() {
    if (firstReelResult == secondReelResult &&
        secondReelResult == thirdReelResult) {
        betResult.text = "JACKPOT!";
        credits += betAmount * 50;
    } else if (firstReelResult == 0 &&
            thirdReelResult == 0) {
        betResult.text =
            "YOU WIN " + (betAmount/2).ToString();
        credits -= (betAmount/2);
    } else if (firstReelResult == secondReelResult) {
        betResult.text = "AWW... ALMOST JACKPOT!";
    } else if (firstReelResult == thirdReelResult) {
        betResult.text =
            "YOU WIN " + (betAmount*2).ToString();
        credits -= (betAmount*2);
    } else {
        betResult.text = "YOU LOSE!";
        credits -= betAmount;
    }
}
```

In the `checkBet()` method, we designed our slot machine to return 50 times the bet if they hit the jackpot, to lose 50% of their bet if the first and third reels are 0, and to win twice if the first and third reels match with any other symbol.

Then, as in the previous example, we generate values for the three reels in the `FixedUpdate()` method, as shown in the following code:

```
private int PickNumber() {
    // Sum the weights of every state.
    var weightSum =
        weightedReelPoll.Sum(state => state.weight);
```

```
    var randomNumber =
      UnityEngine.Random.Range(0, weightSum);
    var i = 0;
    while (randomNumber >= 0) {
        var candidate = weightedReelPoll[i];
        randomNumber -= candidate.weight;
        if (randomNumber <= 0) {
            return candidate.number;
        }
        i++;
    }
    // It should not be possible to reach this point!
    throw new Exception("Something is wrong in the
                        selectState algorithm!");
}

void FixedUpdate () {
    if (startSpin) {
        elapsedTime += Time.deltaTime;
        int randomSpinResult =
          Random.Range(0, numberOfSym);
        if (!firstReelSpinned) {
            firstReel.text = randomSpinResult.ToString();
            if (elapsedTime >= spinDuration) {
                int weightedRandom = PickNumber();
                firstReel.text = weightedRandom.ToString();
                firstReelResult = weightedRandom;
                firstReelSpinned = true;
                elapsedTime = 0;
            }
        } else if (!secondReelSpinned) {
            secondReel.text = randomSpinResult.ToString();
            if (elapsedTime >= spinDuration) {
                secondReelResult = randomSpinResult;
                secondReelSpinned = true;
                elapsedTime = 0;
```

```
        }
    }
...
```

For the first reel, we show the real random values as they occur during the spinning period. Once the time is up, we choose the value from the poll that is already populated with symbols according to the probability distribution. So, our zero symbols will have a 30% better chance of occurring than the rest.

In reality, the player is losing on their bets if they get two zero symbols on the first and third reel; however, we make it seem like a win. It's just a lame message here, but this can work if we combine it with nice graphics, maybe even fireworks, and nice winning sound effects.

A near miss

If the first and second reels return the same symbol, we have to provide the near-miss effect to the players by returning the random value to the third reel close to the second one. We can do this by checking the third random spin result first. If the random value is the same as the first and second results, this is a jackpot, and we shouldn't alter the result.

But if it's not, then we should modify the result so that it is close enough to the other two. Check the comments in the following code:

```
else if (!thirdReelSpinned) {
    thirdReel.text = randomSpinResult.ToString();
    if (elapsedTime >= spinDuration) {
        if ((firstReelResult == secondReelResult)
            && randomSpinResult != firstReelResult) {
            // the first two reels have resulted
            // the same symbol
            // but unfortunately the third reel
            // missed
            // so instead of giving a random number
            // we'll return a symbol which is one
            // less than the other 2
            randomSpinResult = firstReelResult - 1;
            if (randomSpinResult < firstReelResult)
                randomSpinResult =
                    firstReelResult - 1;
            if (randomSpinResult > firstReelResult)
```

```
                    randomSpinResult =
                       firstReelResult + 1;
                if (randomSpinResult < 0)
                    randomSpinResult = 0;
                if (randomSpinResult > 9)
                    randomSpinResult = 9;

                thirdReel.text =
                    randomSpinResult.ToString();
                thirdReelResult = randomSpinResult;
            } else {
                int weightedRandom = PickNumber();
                thirdReel.text =
                    weightedRandom.ToString();
                thirdReelResult = weightedRandom;
            }
            startSpin = false;
            elapsedTime = 0;
            firstReelSpinned = false;
            secondReelSpinned = false;
            checkBet();
        }
    }
}
}
```

And if that near miss happens, you should see it, as shown in the following screenshot:

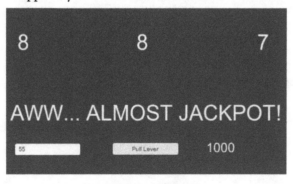

Figure 3.15 – A near miss

We can go even further by adjusting the probability in real time, based on the bet amount (but that'd be too shady). Finally, we can add a **Game Over** message that appears when the player has bet all their money.

This demo shows you the basic implementation of a slot machine game. You can start from this skeleton and improve it with nicer graphics, animations, and sound effects. The important takeaway, though, is understanding that you can already create a game with randomness and probability alone.

Summary

In this chapter, we learned about the applications of probability in AI game design. We experimented with some of the techniques by implementing them in Unity3D. As a bonus, we also learned about how a slot machine works and implemented a simple slot machine game using Unity3D. Probability in games is about making the game, and the characters, seem more realistic by adding uncertainty to their behavior so that players cannot predict the outcome.

In the next chapter, we will look at implementing sensors and how they can make our AI aware of its surroundings.

Further reading

To further study the advanced techniques on probability in games, such as decision making under uncertainty using Bayesian techniques, I recommend reading *AI for Game Developers* by David M. Bourg and Glenn Seeman. *Rules of Play* by Katie Salen is another suggested book on game design.

4

Implementing Sensors

As we discussed in the previous chapter, a character AI system needs to be aware of its surrounding environment. For example, **Non-Player Characters** (**NPCs**) need to know where the obstacles are, the direction the player is looking, whether they are in the player's sight, and a lot more. The quality of the AI of our NPCs depends, for the most part, on the information they can get from the environment. Sensor mistakes are apparent to the player: we've all experienced playing a video game and laughing at an NPC that clearly should have seen us, or, on the other hand, been frustrated because an NPC spotted us from behind a wall.

Video game characters usually get the input information required by their underlying AI decision-making algorithms from sensory information. For simplicity, in this chapter, we will consider *sensory information* as any kind of data coming from the game world. If there's not enough information, characters might show unusual behaviors, such as choosing the wrong places to take cover, idling, or looping in strange actions without knowing how to proceed. A quick search for AI glitches on YouTube opens the door to a vast collection of common funny behaviors of AI, even in AAA games.

In this chapter, we will look at the following topics:

- Introducing sensory systems
- Discovering what a sensory system is and how to implement two senses—sight and touch—in Unity
- Building a demo where we can see our sensory system in action

Technical requirements

For this chapter, you just need Unity3D 2022. You can find the example project described in this chapter in the Chapter 4 folder in the book repository: https://github.com/PacktPublishing/Unity-Artificial-Intelligence-Programming-Fifth-Edition/tree/main/Chapter04.

Basic sensory systems

An AI sensory system emulates senses such as sight, hearing, and even smell to get information from other GameObjects. In such a system, the NPCs need to examine the environment and check for such senses periodically based on their particular interest.

In a minimal sensory system, we have two principal elements: **aspect** (also called **event emitters**) and **sense** (also called **event senses**). Every sense can perceive only a specific aspect; for instance, an NPC with just the sense of hearing can only perceive the sound (one of the aspects) emitted by another GameObject, or a zombie NPC can use its sense of smell to prey on the player's brain. As in real life, we do not need a single sense for every NPC; they can have sight, smell, and touch all at once.

In our demo, we'll implement a base interface, called Sense, that we'll use to implement custom senses. In this chapter, we'll implement sight and touch senses. Sight is what we use to see the world around them; if our AI character sees an enemy, we receive an event in our code, and we act accordingly by doing some action in response. Likewise, with touch, when an enemy gets too close, we want to be able to sense that. Finally, we'll implement a minimal Aspect class that our senses can perceive.

Setting up our scene

Let's get started by setting up our scene:

1. First, we add a plane as a floor.

2. Let's create a few walls to block the line of sight from our AI character to the enemy. We make these out of short—but wide—cubes that we group under an empty GameObject called **Obstacles**.

3. Finally, we add a directional light to see what is going on in our scene.

We represent the player with a tank, similar to what we used earlier, and we represent the NPCs with simple cubes. We also have a **Target** object to show us where the tank is moving in our scene. Our Scene hierarchy should look similar to the following screenshot:

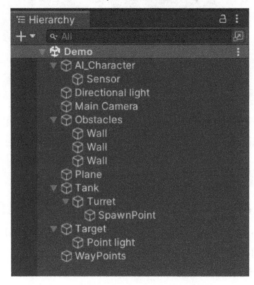

Figure 4.1 – The setup of the example's Hierarchy

Now, let's position the tank, AI character, and walls randomly in our scene. First, make sure to increase the size of the plane to something that looks good. Fortunately, in this demo, all the objects are locked on the plane, and there is no simulated gravity so that nothing can fall off the plane. Also, be sure to adjust the camera so that we can have a clear view of the following scene:

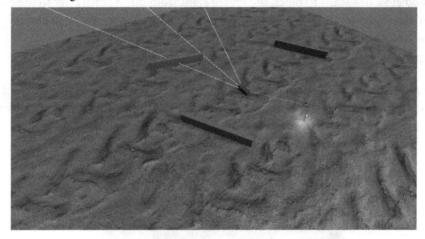

Figure 4.2 – The space that our tank and player wander in

Now that we have the basics set up, let's look at how to implement the tank, AI character, and aspects for our player character.

The player's tank and the aspect class

The **Target** object is a simple sphere object with the mesh render disabled. We have also created a point light and made it a child of our Target object. Make sure that the light is centered, or it will not be very helpful.

Look at the following code in the `Target.cs` file:

```
using UnityEngine;
public class Target : MonoBehaviour {
    [SerializeField]
    private float hOffset = 0.2f;

    void Update () {
        int button = 0;

        //Get the point of the hit position when the mouse
```

```
            //is being clicked
        if(Input.GetMouseButtonDown(button)) {
            Ray ray = Camera.main.ScreenPointToRay(
              Input.mousePosition);
            RaycastHit hitInfo;
            if (Physics.Raycast(ray.origin, ray.direction,
                out hitInfo)) {
                Vector3 targetPosition = hitInfo.point;
                transform.position = targetPosition +
                  new Vector3(0.0f, hOffset, 0.0f);
            }
        }
    }
}
```

Attach this script to the Target object. The script detects the mouse-click event and then, using the raycasting technique, detects the mouse-click location on the plane in the 3D space, and updates the Target object's position in our scene. We will have a look at the player's tank in the following section.

The player's tank

The player's tank is the simple model we used in *Chapter 2*, *Finite State Machines*, with a non-kinematic `Rigidbody` component. We need the `Rigidbody` component to generate trigger events whenever we do collision detection with AI characters and environment objects. Finally, we need to assign the **Player** tag to our tank.

As we can easily see from its name, the `PlayerTank` script controls the player's tank. The following is the code for the `PlayerTank.cs` file:

```
using UnityEngine;

public class PlayerTank : MonoBehaviour {
    public Transform targetTransform;

    [SerializeField]
    private float movementSpeed = 10.0f;
```

```
    [SerializeField]
    private float rotSpeed = 2.0f;


    [SerializeField]
    private float targerReactionRadius = 5.0f;


    void Update () {
        //Stop once you reached near the target position
        if (Vector3.Distance(transform.position,
          targetTransform.position) < targetReactionRadius)
          return;


        //Calculate direction vector from current position
        // to target position


        Vector3 tarPos = targetTransform.position;
        tarPos.y = transform.position.y;
        Vector3 dirRot = tarPos - transform.position;


        //Build a Quaternion for this new rotation vector
        //using LookRotation method
        Quaternion tarRot =
          Quaternion.LookRotation(dirRot);


        //Move and rotate with interpolation
        transform.rotation= Quaternion.Slerp(
          transform.rotation, tarRot,
          rotSpeed * Time.deltaTime);


        transform.Translate(new Vector3(0, 0,
          movementSpeed * Time.deltaTime));
    }
}
```

This script retrieves the Target position on the map and updates the tank's destination point and direction accordingly. The result of the preceding code is shown in the following panel:

Figure 4.3 – The properties of our Tank object

After we assign the preceding script to the tank, be sure to assign the Target object to the targetTransform variable.

Aspect

Next, let's take a look at the `Aspect` class. `Aspect` is an elementary class with just one public property, called `aspectName`. That's all the variables we need in this chapter.

Whenever our AI character senses something, we'll check this against `aspectName` to see whether it's the aspect that the AI has been looking for:

```
using UnityEngine;

public class Aspect : MonoBehaviour {
    public enum Affiliation {
        Player,
        Enemy
    }
    public Affiliation affiliation;
}
```

Attach this aspect script to our player's tank and set the `aspectName` property as `Player`.

AI characters

In this example, the AI characters roam around the scene in a random direction. They have two senses: sight and touch. The sight sense checks whether the enemy aspect is within a set visible range and distance. Touch detects whether the enemy aspect has collided with the `Box Collider` around the character. As we have seen previously, our player's tank has the `Player` aspect. Consequently, these senses are triggered when they detect the player's tank.

For now, let's look at the script we use to move the NPCs around:

```
using UnityEngine;
using System.Collections;

public class Wander : MonoBehaviour {
    private Vector3 tarPos;
```

```
[SerializeField]
private float movementSpeed = 5.0f;

[SerializeField]
private float rotSpeed = 2.0f;

[SerializeField]
private float minX = -45.0f;

[SerializeField]
private float maxX = 45.0f;

[SerializeField]
private float minZ = -45.0f;

[SerializeField]
private float maxZ = -45.0f;

[SerializeField]
private float targetReactionRadius = 5.0f;

[SerializeField]
private float targetVerticalOffset = 0.5f;

void Start () {
    //Get Wander Position
    GetNextPosition();
}

void Update () {
    // Check if we're near the destination position
    if (Vector3.Distance(tarPos, transform.position) <=
        targetReactionRadius) GetNextPosition();
    // generate new random position
```

```
        // Set up quaternion for rotation toward
        // destination
        Quaternion tarRot = Quaternion.LookRotation(
          tarPos - transform.position);


        // Update rotation and translation
        transform.rotation = Quaternion.Slerp(
          transform.rotation,
          tarRot, rotSpeed * Time.deltaTime);

        transform.Translate(new Vector3(0, 0, movementSpeed
                            * Time.deltaTime));
    }

    void GetNextPosition() {
        tarPos = new Vector3(Random.Range(minX, maxX),
          targetVerticalOffset, Random.Range(minZ, maxZ));
    }
}
```

The Wander script generates a new random position in a specified range whenever an AI character reaches its current destination point. Then, the Update method rotates the NPCs and moves them toward their new destination. Attach this script to our AI character so that it can move around in the scene.

Sense

The Sense class is the interface of our sensory system that the other custom senses can implement. It defines two virtual methods, Initialize and UpdateSense, executed from the Start and Update methods, respectively, and that we can override when implementing custom senses as shown in the following code block:

```
using UnityEngine;

public class Sense : MonoBehaviour {
```

```
public bool bDebug = true;
public Aspect.Affiliation targetAffiliation =
   Aspect.Affiliation.Enemy;
public float detectionRate = 1.0f;


protected float elapsedTime = 0.0f;


protected virtual void Initialize() { }
protected virtual void UpdateSense() { }


void Start () {
    Initialize();
}


void Update () {
    UpdateSense();
}
}
```

The basic properties of this script are the intervals between two consecutive sensing operations and the name of the aspect it should look for. This script is not attached to any objects; instead, we use it as a base for specific senses, such as Sight and Touch.

Sight

The Sight sense detects whether a specific aspect is within the perception field of the character. If it perceives anything, it takes the specified action as shown in the following code block:

```
using UnityEngine;


public class Sight: Sense {
    public int FieldOfView = 45;
    public int ViewDistance = 100;


    private Transform playerTrans;
```

```csharp
    private Vector3 rayDirection;


protected override void Initialize() {


    //Find player position
    playerTrans = GameObject.FindGameObjectWithTag(
      "Player").transform;
}


protected override void UpdateSense() {
    elapsedTime += Time.deltaTime;


    // Detect perspective sense if within the detection
    // rate
    if (elapsedTime >= detectionRate) {
        DetectAspect();
        elapsedTime = 0.0f;
    }
}


//Detect perspective field of view for the AI Character
void DetectAspect() {


    //Direction from current position to player
    //position
    rayDirection = (playerTrans.position -
                    transform.position).normalized;


    //Check the angle between the AI character's
    //forward vector and the direction vector between
    //player and AI to detect if the Player is in the
    //field of view.
    if ((Vector3.Angle(rayDirection,
        transform.forward)) < FieldOfView) {
        RaycastHit hit;
        if (Physics.Raycast(transform.position,
```

```
                       rayDirection, out hit, ViewDistance)) {
               Aspect aspect =
                 hit.collider.GetComponent<Aspect>();

               if (aspect != null) {
                   //Check the aspect
                   if (aspect.affiliation ==
                       targetAffiliation) {
                       print("Enemy Detected");
                   }
               }
           }
       }
   }
```

We need to implement the Initialize and UpdateSense methods of the parent Sense class, respectively. Then, in the DetectAspect method, we first check the angle between the player and the AI's current direction. Then, if it's in the field-of-view range, we shoot a ray in the direction of the player's tank. The length of the ray is the value in the visible distance property.

The Raycast method returns when it first hits another object. Then, we check this against the aspect component and the aspect name. In this way, even if the player is in the visible range, the AI character will not see the player if they hide behind a wall.

The OnDrawGizmos method draws lines based on the perspective field (determined by the view angle and viewing distance) to see the AI character's line of sight in the editor window during playtesting. Attach this script to the AI character, and ensure to set the aspect name to Enemy.

This method can be illustrated as follows:

```
void OnDrawGizmos() {
    if (!Application.isEditor|| playerTrans == null)
      return;
    Debug.DrawLine(transform.position,
                   playerTrans.position, Color.red);
    Vector3 frontRayPoint = transform.position +
      (transform.forward * ViewDistance);
```

```
        //Approximate perspective visualization
        Vector3 leftRayPoint = Quaternion.Euler(
           0,FieldOfView * 0.5f ,0) * frontRayPoint;
        Vector3 rightRayPoint = Quaternion.Euler(0,
           - FieldOfView*0.5f, 0) * frontRayPoint;
        Debug.DrawLine(transform.position, frontRayPoint,
                       Color.green);
        Debug.DrawLine(transform.position, leftRayPoint,
                       Color.green);
        Debug.DrawLine(transform.position, rightRayPoint,
                       Color.green);
    }
}
```

OnDrawGizmos is an event function that we can use when we want to draw gizmos in the scene. **Gizmos** are visual debug aids that will only be rendered in the Scene view (and are invisible in the normal Game view). In it, we can use gizmo functions such as DrawLine, DrawIcon, and DrawSphere.

They are a handy way to quickly provide some visual feedback to our algorithms. You can learn more about the gizmo functions by following this link: https://docs.unity3d.com/ScriptReference/Gizmos.html.

Touch

Another sense we're going to implement is Touch, which is triggered when the player entity is within a specific range of the AI entity as shown in the following code block. Our AI character has a box collider component, and its Is Trigger flag is on:

```
using UnityEngine;

public class Touch : Sense {
    void OnTriggerEnter(Collider other) {
```

```
        Aspect aspect = other.GetComponent<Aspect>();
        if (aspect != null) {
            //Check the aspect
            if (aspect.affiliation == targetAffiliation) {
                print("Enemy Touch Detected");
            }
        }
    }
}
```

We need to implement the OnTriggerEnter event fired whenever the collider component collides with another collider component. Since our tank entity also has collider and Rigidbody components, a collision event occurs as soon as the colliders of the AI character and the player's tank coincide.

The following screenshot shows the box collider of our enemy AI that we are using to implement the Touch sense:

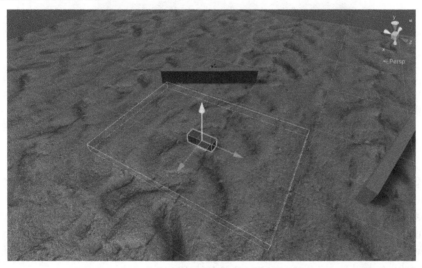

Figure 4.4 – The collider component around our player

In the following screenshot, we can see how our AI character is set up:

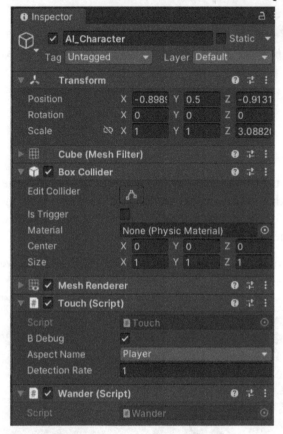

Figure 4.5 – Properties of our player

Inside the OnTriggerEnter method, we access the aspect component of the other collider entity and check whether the name of the aspect is the same aspect that this AI character is looking for. For demonstration purposes, we print out in the console that the character detects the enemy aspect by the Touch sense. In a real game, we would not print the event but rather trigger other actions, such as turning to face an enemy and then chasing, attacking, and so on. Let's move on to testing our game.

Testing the game

Now, play the game in Unity3D and move the player's tank near the wandering AI character by clicking on the ground. You should see the **Enemy touch detected** message in the console log window whenever our AI character gets close to our player's tank.

Figure 4.6 – Our player and tank in action

The previous screenshot shows an AI agent with touch and perspective senses looking for an enemy aspect. Move the player's tank in front of the AI character, and you'll get the *Enemy detected* message. If you go into the editor view while running the game, you should see the rendered debug drawings thanks to the OnDrawGizmos method implemented in the Sight sense class.

Summary

This chapter introduced the concept of using sensors in implementing game AI, and we implemented two senses, Sight and Touch, for our AI character. The sensory system is just the first element of the decision-making system of a whole AI system. For example, we can use the sensory system to control the execution of a behavior system or change the state of a Finite State Machine once we have detected an enemy within the AI's line of sight.

We will cover how to apply behavior tree systems in *Chapter 9, Behavior Trees*. In the meantime, in the next chapter, we'll look at how to implement flocking behaviors in Unity3D, as well as how to implement Craig Reynold's flocking algorithm.

Part 2: Movement and Navigation

In this part, we will learn how to make characters move and find paths through game environments.

We will cover the following chapters in this part:

- *Chapter 5, Flocking*
- *Chapter 6, Path Following and Steering Behaviors*
- *Chapter 7, A* Pathfinding*
- *Chapter 8, Navigation Mesh*

5
Flocking

During early summer evenings, you have probably seen flocks of birds flying in the sky. You have probably noted how they seem to move as a single living object: they all move in a particular direction, turn around, and grow and shrink. A flocking system aims to replicate this behavior in games: we want to implement an algorithm to move many objects as an organic group.

In games, we call each element of a flock a **boid**. To implement a flocking behavior, we do not need to equip each boid with a high-level complex decision-making system; instead, all we need to do is implement simple *reactive* rules for each boid that depend only on the state of the flock itself. Thus, flocking is an excellent example of emergent behavior: each boid reacts exclusively to its neighbor's behaviors; nevertheless, the flock seems to move as if someone were coordinating it.

In this chapter, we will learn what these rules are and how to implement them in Unity3D. We will implement two variations of flocking in this chapter. The first one is based on an old flocking behavior demo that has been circulating in the Unity community since since the game engine was created.

The second variation is based on Craig Reynold's original flocking algorithm from 1986.

In this chapter, we will cover the following topics:

- An overview of basic flocking behavior and how to implement it
- An alternative implementation of flocking behavior

Technical requirements

For this chapter, you just need Unity3D 2022. You can find the example project described in this chapter in the Chapter 5 folder in the book's repository: https://github.com/PacktPublishing/Unity-Artificial-Intelligence-Programming-Fifth-Edition/tree/main/Chapter05.

Basic flocking behavior

As we said in the introduction to this chapter, we can describe a flocking behavior by using just three intuitive properties:

- **Separation**: This property, also called *short-range repulsion*, represents the minimum distance between neighboring boids to avoid collisions. You can imagine this rule as a force that pushes a boid away from the others.

- **Alignment**: This property represents the likelihood for each boid to move in the same direction as the flock (we measure this as the average direction of all the individual boids).

- **Cohesion**: This property, also called *long-range attraction*, represents the likelihood for each boid to move toward the center of mass of the flock (we measure this by averaging the position of each boid in the flock). Thus, you can imagine this rule as a force that pushes a boid toward the center of the flock.

In this demo, we will create a scene with flocks of objects and implement the flocking behavior in C#. For this first version, we compute all the rules by ourselves. Also, we will create a boid commander that leads the crowd to control and track the general position of the flock easily.

You can see the **Hierarchy** scene in the following screenshot. As you can see, we have several boid entities named **UnityFlock**, under a controller named **UnityFlockController**. **UnityFlock** entities are individual boid objects that refer to their parent **UnityFlockController** entity, using it as a leader. The controller updates the next destination point randomly once it reaches the current destination point:

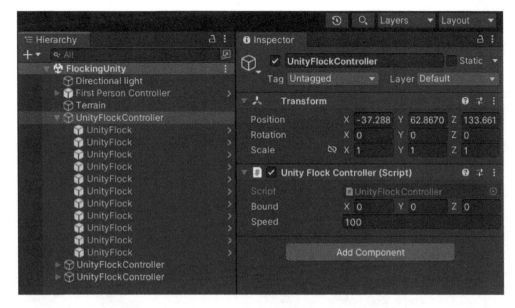

Figure 5.1 – The scene hierarchy

UnityFlock is a prefab with just a cube mesh and a `UnityFlock` script. We can use any other mesh representation for this prefab to represent something more interesting, such as birds. You can add as many **UnityFlock** prefabs as you like. The algorithm will automatically check the number of children in the **UnityFlockController** object.

Individual behavior

Boid is a term coined by Craig Reynold that refers to bird-like objects. We use this term to describe each object in our flock. The boid behaviour consists of a group of objects, each having their individual position, velocity, and orientation. Now, let's implement the boid behavior. You can find the behavior that controls each boid in the flock in the `UnityFlock.cs` script, which we'll examine now:

```
using UnityEngine;
using System.Collections;

public class UnityFlock : MonoBehaviour {
    public float minSpeed = 20.0f;
    public float turnSpeed = 20.0f;
    public float randomFreq = 20.0f;
```

```
public float randomForce = 20.0f;


//alignment variables
public float toOriginForce = 50.0f;
public float toOriginRange = 100.0f;


public float gravity = 2.0f;


//seperation variables
public float avoidanceRadius = 50.0f;
public float avoidanceForce = 20.0f;


//cohesion variables
public float followVelocity = 4.0f;
public float followRadius = 40.0f;


//these variables control the movement of the boid
private Transform origin;


private Vector3 velocity;
private Vector3 normalizedVelocity;
private Vector3 randomPush;
private Vector3 originPush;
private Transform[] objects;
private UnityFlock[] otherFlocks;
private Transform transformComponent;
private float randomFreqInterval;
```

As public fields, we declare the input values for our algorithm. These can be set up and customized from within the Inspector. In this script, we perform the following operations:

1. We define the minimum movement speed (minSpeed) and rotation speed (turnSpeed) for our boid.

2. We use randomFreq to determine how many times we want to update the randomPush value, based on the randomForce value. Then, we use this force to vary the single boid's velocity and make the flock's movement look more realistic.

3. `toOriginRange` specifies how much we want the flock to spread out. In other words, it represents the maximum distance from the flock's origin in which we want to maintain the boids (following the previously mentioned cohesion rule). We use the `avoidanceRadius` and `avoidanceForce` properties to maintain a minimum distance between individual boids (following the separation rule). Similarly, we use `followRadius` and `followVelocity` to keep a minimum distance between the leader or origin of the flock. The `origin` variable stores the parent object that controls the entire flock; in other words, it is the flock leader. The boids need to know about the other boids in the flock. Therefore, we use the `objects` and `otherFlocks` attributes to store the neighboring boid's information.

This is the initialization method for our boid:

```
void Start () {
    randomFreqInterval = 1.0f / randomFreq;

    // Assign the parent as origin
    origin = transform.parent;

    // Flock transform
    transformComponent = transform;

    // Temporary components
    Component[] tempFlocks= null;

    // Get all the unity flock components from the parent
    // transform in the group
    if (transform.parent) {
        tempFlocks = transform.parent
            .GetComponentsInChildren<UnityFlock>();
    }
    // Assign and store all the flock objects in this group
    objects = new Transform[tempFlocks.Length];
    otherFlocks = new UnityFlock[tempFlocks.Length];

    for (int i = 0;i<tempFlocks.Length;i++) {
        objects[i] = tempFlocks[i].transform;
        otherFlocks[i] = (UnityFlock)tempFlocks[i];
```

```
    }

    // Null Parent as the flock leader will be
    // UnityFlockController object
    transform.parent = null;

    // Calculate random push depends on the random
    // frequency provided
    StartCoroutine(UpdateRandom());
}
```

We set the parent of the object of our boid as origin, meaning that this is the controller object for the other boids to follow. Then, we grab all the other boids in the group and store them in the `otherFlocks` attribute for later reference.

> **Coroutines**
>
> Put simply, coroutines are *functions that can be paused*. With coroutines, you can run a method, pause the execution for a desired amount of time (for example, a single frame or several seconds), and then continue from the following line as if nothing happened. They have two primary use cases: to run a function after a specific interval (without keeping track of every frame of `elapsedTimes`, as we did in other examples) or to split the computation of some heavy algorithm over multiple frames (and, therefore, not incur in frame drops). Coroutines, it turns out, are a pretty helpful tool to master. You can read more at `https://docs.unity3d.com/Manual/Coroutines.html`.

Now, we can implement the `UpdateRandom` coroutine. As a coroutine, the function never actually terminates, but we run the body of the `while` loop for each random time interval:

1. We define the `UpdateRandom` method as a coroutine by specifying the `IEnumerator` return type:

```
IEnumerator UpdateRandom() {
    while (true) {
        randomPush =
            Random.insideUnitSphere * randomForce;
        yield return new WaitForSeconds(
            randomFreqInterval + Random.Range(
```

```
                -randomFreqInterval / 2.0f,
                randomFreqInterval / 2.0f));
       }
   }
```

2. The `UpdateRandom()` method updates the `randomPush` value throughout the game with an interval based on `randomFreq`. `Random.insideUnitSphere` returns a `Vector3` object with random *x*, *y*, and *z* values within a sphere, with a radius of the `randomForce` value.

3. We wait for a certain random amount of time before resuming `while(true)`.

4. Loop to update the `randomPush` value again.

5. Now, here is our boid behavior's `Update()` method, which helps the boid entity comply with the three rules of the flocking algorithm:

```
void Update() {
        //Internal variables
        float speed = velocity.magnitude;
        Vector3 avgVelocity = Vector3.zero;
        Vector3 avgPosition = Vector3.zero;
        int count = 0;

        Vector3 myPosition =
          transformComponent.position;
        Vector3 forceV;
        Vector3 toAvg;

        for (int i = 0; i < objects.Length; i++) {
            Transform boidTransform = objects[i];
            if (boidTransform != transformComponent) {
                Vector3 otherPosition =
                  boidTransform.position;

                // Average position to calculate
                // cohesion
                avgPosition += otherPosition;
                count++;
```

```
//Directional vector from other flock
// to this flock
forceV = myPosition - otherPosition;

//Magnitude of that directional
//vector(Length)
float directionMagnitude =
  forceV.magnitude;
float forceMagnitude = 0.0f;

if (directionMagnitude < followRadius)
{
    if (directionMagnitude <
        avoidanceRadius) {
        forceMagnitude = 1.0f -
          (directionMagnitude /
          avoidanceRadius);

        if (directionMagnitude > 0)
            avgVelocity += (forceV /
              directionMagnitude) *
              forceMagnitude *
              avoidanceForce;
    }

    forceMagnitude =
      directionMagnitude /
      followRadius;
    UnityFlock tempOtherBoid =
      otherFlocks[i];
    avgVelocity += followVelocity *
      forceMagnitude *
      tempOtherBoid.normalizedVelocity;
    }
  }
}
```

The preceding code implements the separation rule. First, we check the distance between the current boid and the other boids, and then we update the velocity accordingly, as explained in the comments in the preceding code block.

6. We now calculate the average velocity vector of the flock by dividing the current velocity vector by the number of boids in the flock:

```
if (count > 0) {
    //Calculate the average flock
    //velocity(Alignment)
    avgVelocity /= count;

    //Calculate Center value of the
    //flock(Cohesion)
    toAvg = (avgPosition / count) -
        myPosition;
} else {
    toAvg = Vector3.zero;
}

//Directional Vector to the leader
forceV = origin.position - myPosition;
float leaderDirectionMagnitude =
    forceV.magnitude;
float leaderForceMagnitude =
    leaderDirectionMagnitude / toOriginRange;

//Calculate the velocity of the flock to the
//leader
if (leaderDirectionMagnitude > 0)
    originPush = leaderForceMagnitude *
        toOriginForce * (forceV /
        leaderDirectionMagnitude);

if (speed < minSpeed && speed > 0) {
    velocity = (velocity / speed) * minSpeed;
}
```

```
        Vector3 wantedVel = velocity;

        //Calculate final velocity
        wantedVel -= wantedVel * Time.deltaTime;
        wantedVel += randomPush * Time.deltaTime;
        wantedVel += originPush * Time.deltaTime;
        wantedVel += avgVelocity * Time.deltaTime;
        wantedVel += gravity * Time.deltaTime *
          toAvg.normalized;

        velocity = Vector3.RotateTowards(velocity,
          wantedVel, turnSpeed * Time.deltaTime,
          100.00f);
        transformComponent.rotation =
          Quaternion.LookRotation(velocity);

        //Move the flock based on the calculated
        //velocity
        transformComponent.Translate(velocity *
          Time.deltaTime, Space.World);

        normalizedVelocity = velocity.normalized;
    }
```

7. We add up all the factors, such as randomPush, originPush, and avgVelocity, to calculate the final target velocity vector, wantedVel. We also update the current velocity to wantedVel with a linear interpolation by using the Vector3.RotateTowards method.

8. We move our boid based on the new velocity using the Translate method.

9. As a final touch, we create a cube mesh, to which we add the `UnityFlock` script, and then save it as a prefab, as shown in the following screenshot:

Figure 5.2 – The UnityFlock prefab

Controller

Now, it is time to create the controller class. This class updates its position so that the other individual boid objects know where to go. The `origin` variable in the preceding `UnityFlock` script contains a reference to this object.

The following is the code in the `UnityFlockController.cs` file:

```
using UnityEngine;
using System.Collections;

public class UnityFlockController : MonoBehaviour {
    public Vector3 bound;
    public float speed = 100.0f;
    public float targetReachedRadius = 10.0f;

    private Vector3 initialPosition;
    private Vector3 nextMovementPoint;

    // Use this for initialization
    void Start () {
        initialPosition = transform.position;
        CalculateNextMovementPoint();
    }

    // Update is called once per frame
    void Update () {
        transform.Translate(Vector3.forward * speed *
          Time.deltaTime);
        transform.rotation =
          Quaternion.Slerp(transform.rotation,
            Quaternion.LookRotation(nextMovementPoint -
            transform.position), 1.0f * Time.deltaTime);

        if (Vector3.Distance(nextMovementPoint,
            transform.position) <= targetReachedRadius)
            CalculateNextMovementPoint();
    }
```

In the `Update()` method, we check whether our controller object is near the target destination point. If it is, we update the `nextMovementPoint` variable again with the `CalculateNextMovementPoint()` method that we just discussed:

```
void CalculateNextMovementPoint () {
    float posX = Random.Range(initialPosition.x - bound.x,
        initialPosition.x + bound.x);
    float posY = Random.Range(initialPosition.y - bound.y,
        initialPosition.y + bound.y);
    float posZ = Random.Range(initialPosition.z - bound.z,
        initialPosition.z + bound.z);

    nextMovementPoint = initialPosition + new Vector3(posX,
        posY, posZ);
}
```

The `CalculateNextMovementPoint()` method finds the next random destination position in a range between the current position and the boundary vectors.

Finally, we put all of this together, as shown in *Figure 5.1*, which should give you flocks of squares flying around realistically in the sunset:

Figure 5.3 – A demonstration of the flocking behavior using the Unity seagull sample

The previous example gave you the basics of flocking behaviors. In the next section, we will explore a different implementation that makes use of Unity's `Rigidbody` component.

Alternative implementation

In this section, we use the Unity physics engine to simplify the code a bit. In fact, in this example, we attach a `Rigidbody` component to the boids to use the `Rigidbody` properties to translate and steer them. In addition, the `Rigidbody` component is also helpful in preventing the other boids from overlapping with each other.

In this implementation, we have two components: the individual boid behavior and the controller behavior (the element referred to as the *flock controller* in the previous section). As before, the controller is the object that the rest of the boids follow.

The code in the `Flock.cs` file is as follows:

```
using UnityEngine;
using System.Collections;
using System.Collections.Generic;

public class Flock : MonoBehaviour {
    internal FlockController controller;
    private new Rigidbody rigidbody;

    private void Start() {
        rigidbody = GetComponent<Rigidbody>();
    }

    void Update () {
        if (controller) {
            Vector3 relativePos = Steer() * Time.deltaTime;

            if (relativePos != Vector3.zero)
              rigidbody.velocity = relativePos;

            // enforce minimum and maximum speeds for the
            // boids
            float speed = rigidbody.velocity.magnitude;
            if (speed > controller.maxVelocity) {
                rigidbody.velocity =
                    rigidbody.velocity.normalized *
                    controller.maxVelocity;
```

```
            } else if (speed < controller.minVelocity) {
                rigidbody.velocity =
                    rigidbody.velocity.normalized *
                    controller.minVelocity;
            }
        }
    }
```

We will create `FlockController` in a moment. In the meantime, in the `Update()` method in the previous code block, we calculate the boid's velocity using the `Steer()` method and apply the result to the boid's rigid-body velocity.

Next, we check whether the current speed of the `Rigidbody` component falls inside our controller's maximum and minimum velocity ranges. If not, we cap the velocity at the preset range:

```
private Vector3 Steer () {
    Vector3 center = controller.flockCenter -
        transform.localPosition;    // cohesion

    Vector3 velocity = controller.flockVelocity -
        rigidbody.velocity; // allignement

    Vector3 follow = controller.target.localPosition -
        transform.localPosition; // follow leader

    Vector3 separation = Vector3.zero;

    foreach (Flock flock in controller.flockList) {
        if (flock != this) {
            Vector3 relativePos = transform.localPosition -
                flock.transform.localPosition;

            separation += relativePos.normalized;
        }
    }

    // randomize
```

```
Vector3 randomize = new Vector3( (Random.value * 2) -
    1, (Random.value * 2) - 1, (Random.value * 2) - 1);
randomize.Normalize();


return (controller.centerWeight * center +
        controller.velocityWeight * velocity +
        controller.separationWeight * separation +
        controller.followWeight * follow +
        controller.randomizeWeight * randomize);
}
```

The steer() method implements the *separation*, *cohesion*, *alignment*, and *follows the leader* rules of the flocking algorithm. Then, we add up all the factors with a random weight value. We use this *Flock* script together with the Rigidbody and SphereCollider components to create a Flock prefab, as shown in the following screenshot (make sure to disable the gravity by unchecking **Use Gravity**):

Figure 5.4 – Flock

It is now time to implement the final piece of the puzzle: the FlockController component.

FlockController

This `FlockController` component is similar to the one in the previous example. In addition to controlling the flock's speed and position, this script also instantiates the boids at runtime:

1. The code in the `FlockController.cs` file is as follows:

```
using UnityEngine;
using System.Collections;
using System.Collections.Generic;

public class FlockController : MonoBehaviour {
    public float minVelocity = 1;
    public float maxVelocity = 8;
    public int flockSize = 20;

    public float centerWeight = 1;
    public float velocityWeight = 1;
    public float separationWeight = 1;
    public float followWeight = 1;
    public float randomizeWeight = 1;

    public Flock prefab;
    public Transform target;

    Vector3 flockCenter;
    internal Vector3 flockVelocity;
    public ArrayList flockList = new ArrayList();

    void Start () {
        for (int i = 0; i < flockSize; i++) {
            Flock flock = Instantiate(prefab,
                transform.position, transform.rotation)
                as Flock;
            flock.transform.parent = transform;
            flock.controller = this;
            flockList.Add(flock);
```

```
        }
    }
```

2. We declare all the public properties to implement the flocking algorithm and then start generating the boid objects based on the flock size input.

3. We set up the controller class and the parent `Transform` object, as we did last time.

4. We add every boid object we create to the `flockList` array. The target variable accepts an entity to be used as a moving leader. In this example, we create a sphere entity as a moving target leader for our flock:

```
void Update() {
    //Calculate the Center and Velocity of the
    // whole flock group
    Vector3 center = Vector3.zero;
    Vector3 velocity = Vector3.zero;

    foreach (Flock flock in flockList) {
        center +=
            flock.transform.localPosition;
        velocity += flock.GetComponent
        <Rigidbody>().velocity;
    }

    flockCenter = center / flockSize;
    flockVelocity = velocity / flockSize;
    }
}
```

5. In the `Update` method, we keep updating the average center and velocity of the flock. These are the values referenced from the boid object and are used to adjust the cohesion and alignment properties with the controller:

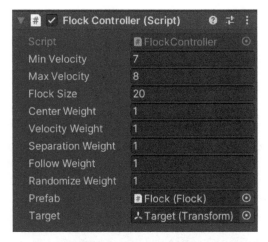

Figure 5.5 – Flock Controller

We need to implement our **Target** entity with the **Target Movement (Script)**. The movement script is the same as what we saw in our previous Unity3D sample controller's movement script:

Figure 5.6 – The Target entity with the TargetMovement script

6. Here is how our `TargetMovement` script works: we pick a random point nearby for the target to move to, and when we get close to that point, we pick a new one. The code in the `TargetMovement.cs` file is as follows:

```
using UnityEngine;
using System.Collections;

public class TargetMovement : MonoBehaviour {
    // Move target around circle with tangential speed
    public Vector3 bound;
    public float speed = 100.0f;
    public float targetReachRadius = 10.0f;
    private Vector3 initialPosition;
    private Vector3 nextMovementPoint;

    void Start () {
        initialPosition = transform.position;
        CalculateNextMovementPoint();
    }

    void CalculateNextMovementPoint () {
        float posX = Random.Range(initialPosition.x =
            bound.x, initialPosition.x+bound.x);
        float posY = Random.Range(initialPosition.y =
            bound.y, initialPosition.y+bound.y);
        float posZ = Random.Range(initialPosition.z =
            bound.z, initialPosition.z+bound.z);

        nextMovementPoint = initialPosition +
            new Vector3(posX, posY, posZ);
    }

    void Update () {
        transform.Translate(Vector3.forward * speed *
            Time.deltaTime);
```

```
transform.rotation =
    Quaternion.Slerp(transform.rotation,
    Quaternion.LookRotation(nextMovementPoint -
    transform.position), Time.deltaTime);

    if (Vector3.Distance(nextMovementPoint,
    transform.position) <= targetReachRadius)
    CalculateNextMovementPoint();
    }
}
```

7. After we put everything together, we should see a nice flock of cubic boids flying around in the scene, all chasing the spheric target:

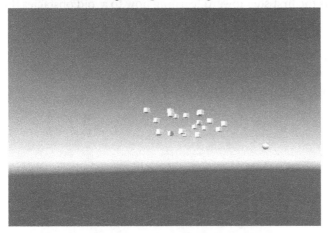

Figure 5.7 – Flocking with Craig Reynold's algorithm

Now that we have implemented flocking behavior in two different ways, we can experiment with different parameters and tweak the boids' behavior until we find a movement we like. I want to conclude this chapter with an important takeaway: note that we do not need complex algorithms to have a natural-looking behavior. For that, we just need simple reactive rules and a way to combine them.

Summary

In this chapter, we learned how to implement flocking behaviors in two ways. First, we examined and learned how to implement a basic flocking algorithm using nothing other than our scripts. Next, we implemented the same algorithm using Unity's `Rigidbody` component to control the boid's movement and Sphere Collider to avoid collision with other boids.

In our example, we always referred to boids as bird-like entities. However, we can use flocking for many other applications: fishes swimming in the sea, sheep grazing on a plane, a swarm of insects, and even groups of people walking on the street can show flocking behavior. To adapt the algorithm to different scenarios, we just need to change the flocking rules' values and eventually lock the movement to a plane.

In the next chapter, we will go beyond random movement and look at how to follow a specific path. This is the first step toward learning how to avoid obstacles that are in your way.

6
Path Following and Steering Behaviors

In this short chapter, we will implement two Unity3D demos to explore steering behaviors. In the first demo, we will implement a script to make an entity follow a simple path. In the second demo, we will set up a scene with a couple of obstacles and program an entity to reach a target while avoiding the obstacles.

Obstacle avoidance is a fundamental behavior for game characters when moving around and interacting with the game world. However, obstacle avoidance is generally used with other navigation systems (such as pathfinding or crowd simulations). In this chapter, we will use the systems to make sure that we avoid the other agents and reach the target. We will not talk about how fast the character will reach a destination, and we will not calculate the shortest path to the target, as we'll talk about these in the next chapter.

In this chapter, we'll look at the following two fundamental aspects of movement:

- Following a path
- Avoiding obstacles

Technical requirements

For this chapter, you just need Unity3D 2022. You can find the example project described in this chapter in the Chapter 6 folder in the book repository: https://github. com/PacktPublishing/Unity-Artificial-Intelligence-Programming-Fifth-Edition/tree/main/Chapter06.

Following a path

A **path** is a sequence of points in the game, connecting a point *A* to a point *B*. There are many ways to build a path. Usually, a path is generated by other game systems such as *pathfinding* (see *Chapter 7, A* Pathfinding*); however, in our demo, we construct the path by hand using waypoints. So first, we write a Path.cs script that takes a list of game objects as waypoints and create a path out of them.

Path script

Let's look at the path script responsible for managing the path for our objects. Consider the following code in the Path.cs file:

```csharp
using UnityEngine;

public class Path : MonoBehaviour {
    public bool isDebug = true;
    public Transform[] waypoints;

    public float Length {
        get {
            return waypoints.Length;
        }
    }

    public Vector3 GetPoint(int index) {
        return waypoints[index].position;
    }

    void OnDrawGizmos() {
        if (!isDebug)
            return;
```

```
for (int i = 1; i < waypoints.Length; i++) {
        Debug.DrawLine(waypoints[i-1].position,
        waypoints[i].position, Color.red);
    }
    }
}
```

As you can see, that is a straightforward script. It has a `Length` property that returns the number of waypoints. The `GetPoint` method returns the position of a particular waypoint at a specified index in the array. Then, we have the `OnDrawGizmos` method called by the Unity3D frame to draw components in the editor environment. The drawing here won't be rendered in the game view unless the gizmos flag, located in the top right corner, is turned on.

Figure 6.1 – The gizmos visibility option in the Editor view

Now let's create the scene. Create an empty **Path** game object and attach to it the **Path** script. Then, let's add to it some empty game objects as children. They will be the waypoints markers.

Figure 6.2 – Here is how we organize the Hierarchy

Select the **Path** object. We now have to fill the **Waypoints** array in the Inspector with the actual waypoint markers. As usual, we can do this by dragging and dropping the game objects from the Hierarchy to the Inspector.

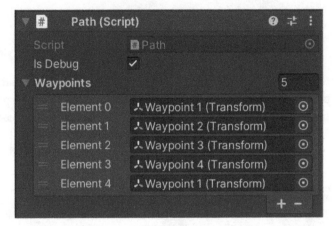

Figure 6.3 – The Path script configuration in the Inspector

The preceding list shows the **Waypoints** in the example project. However, you can move the waypoints around in the editor, use the same waypoint multiple times, or whatever else you like.

The other property is a checkbox to enable the **debug** mode and the waypoint radius. If we enable the **debug** mode property, Unity draws the path formed by connecting the waypoints as a gizmo in the editor view as shown in *Figure 6.4.*

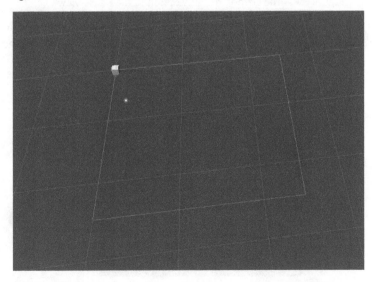

Figure 6.4 – The path's gizmo is drawn in the editor view

Now that we have a path, we need to design a character that can follow it. We do that in the following section.

Path-following agents

For this demo, the main character is represented by a brave and valiant cube. But, of course, the same script applies to whatever 3D models you want.

Let's start by creating a `VehicleFollowing` script. The script takes a couple of parameters: the first is the reference to the path object it needs to follow (the **Path** variable); then, we have the **Speed** and **Mass** properties, which we need to calculate the character's velocity over time. Finally, if checked, the **Is Looping** flag instructs the entity to follow the path continuously in a closed loop.

Let's take a look at the following code in the `VehicleFollowing.cs` file:

```
using UnityEngine;

public class VehicleFollowing : MonoBehaviour {
    public Path path;
    public float speed = 10.0f;

    [Range(1.0f, 1000.0f)]
    public float steeringInertia = 100.0f;

    public bool isLooping = true;
    public float waypointRadius = 1.0f;

    //Actual speed of the vehicle
    private float curSpeed;

    private int curPathIndex = 0;
    private float pathLength;
    private Vector3 targetPoint;

    Vector3 velocity;
```

First, we specify all the script properties. Then, we initialize the properties and set up the starting direction of our velocity vector using the entity's forward vector. We do this in the `Start` method, as shown in the following code:

```
void Start () {
    pathLength = path.Length;
    velocity = transform.forward;
}
```

In this script, there are only two methods that are really important: the `Update` and `Steer` methods. Let's take a look at the first one:

```
void Update() {
    //Unify the speed
    curSpeed = speed * Time.deltaTime;


    targetPoint = path.GetPoint(curPathIndex);

    //If reach the radius of the waypoint then move to
    //next point in the path
    if (Vector3.Distance(transform.position,
        targetPoint) < waypointRadius) {
        //Don't move the vehicle if path is finished
        if (curPathIndex < pathLength - 1)
            curPathIndex++;
        else if (isLooping)
            curPathIndex = 0;
        else
            return;
    }

    //Move the vehicle until the end point is reached
    //in the path
    if (curPathIndex >= pathLength)
        return;

    //Calculate the next Velocity towards the path
    if (curPathIndex >= pathLength - 1 && !isLooping)
```

```
        velocity += Steer(targetPoint, true);
    else
        velocity += Steer(targetPoint);
    //Move the vehicle according to the velocity
    transform.position += velocity;
    //Rotate the vehicle towards the desired Velocity
    transform.rotation =
      Quaternion.LookRotation(velocity);
}
```

In the Update method, we check whether the entity has reached a particular waypoint by calculating if the distance between its current position and the target waypoint is smaller than the waypoint's radius. If it is, we increase the index, setting in this way the target position to the next waypoint in the waypoints array. If it was the last waypoint, we check the isLooping flag.

If it is active, we set the destination to the starting waypoint; otherwise, we stop. An alternative solution is to program it so that our object turns around and goes back the way it came. Implementing this behavior is not a difficult task, so we leave this to the reader as a helpful practice exercise.

Now, we calculate the acceleration and rotation of the entity using the Steer method. In this method, we rotate and update the entity's position according to the speed and direction of the velocity vector:

```
public Vector3 Steer(Vector3 target, bool bFinalPoint =
  false) {
    //Calculate the directional vector from the current
    //position towards the target point
    Vector3 desiredVelocity =
      (target - transform.position);
    float dist = desiredVelocity.magnitude;

    //Normalize the desired Velocity
    desiredVelocity.Normalize();

    //
    if (bFinalPoint && dist < waypointRadius)
        desiredVelocity *=
```

```
                    curSpeed * (dist / waypointRadius);
        else
            desiredVelocity *= curSpeed;


    //Calculate the force Vector
    Vector3 steeringForce = desiredVelocity - velocity;


    return steeringForce / steeringInertia;
    }
}
```

The `Steer` method takes two parameters: the target position and a boolean, which tells us whether this is the final waypoint in the path. As first, we calculate the remaining distance from the current position to the target position. Then we subtract the current position vector from the target position vector to get a vector pointing toward the target position. We are not interested in the vector's size, just in its direction, so we normalize it.

Now, suppose we are moving to the final waypoint, and its distance from us is less than the waypoint radius. In that case, we want to slow down gradually until the velocity becomes zero precisely at the waypoint position so that the character correctly stops in place. Otherwise, we update the target velocity with the desired maximum speed value. Then, in the same way as before, we can calculate the new steering vector by subtracting the current velocity vector from this target velocity vector. Finally, by dividing this vector by the steering inertia value of our entity, we get a smooth steering (note that the minimal value for the steering inertia is `1`, corresponding to instantaneous steering).

Now that we have a script, we can create an empty `Cube` object and put it at the beginning of the path. Then, we add the `VehicleFollowing` script component to it, as shown in the following screenshot:

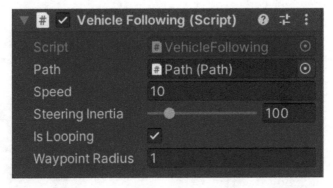

Figure 6.5 – The properties of the VehicleFollowing script

You should see our cubic character follow the path if you run the scene. You can also see the path in the editor view. Play around with the speed and steering inertia values of the cube and radius values of the path, and see how they affect the system's overall behavior.

Avoiding obstacles

In this section, we explore obstacle avoidance. As a first step, we need, of course, obstacles. So, we set up a scene similar to the one shown in *Figure 6.6*. Then, we create a script for the main character to avoid obstacles while trying to reach the target point. The algorithm presented here uses the raycasting method, which is very straightforward. However, this means it can only avoid obstacles that are blocking its path directly in front of it:

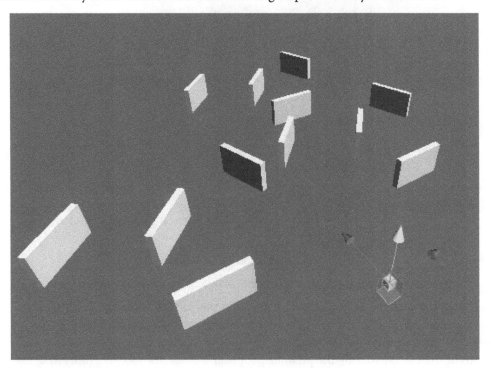

Figure 6.6 – A sample scene setup

We make a few cube entities and group them under an empty game object called `Obstacles` to create the environment. We also create another cube object called `Vehicle` and give it the obstacle avoidance script. Finally, we create a plane object representing the ground.

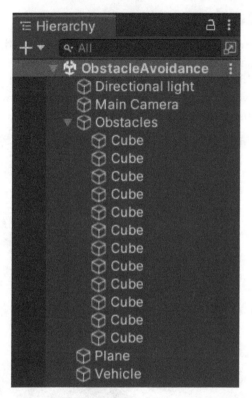

Figure 6.7 – Here is the structure of the scene's Hierarchy

It is worth noting that the **Vehicle** object does not perform pathfinding, that is, the active search for a path to the destination. Instead, it only avoids obstacles locally as it follows the path. Roughly speaking, it is the difference between you planning a path from your home to the mall, and avoiding the possible people and obstacles you may find along the path. As such, if we set too many walls up, the **Vehicle** might have a hard time finding the target: for instance, if the Agent ends up facing a dead-end in a U-shaped object, it may not be able to get out. Try a few different wall setups and see how your agent performs.

Adding a custom layer

We now add a custom layer to the Obstacles object:

1. To add a new layer, navigate to **Edit | Project Settings**:

Figure 6.8 – The Project Settings

2. Go to the **Tags and Layer** section.
3. Assign the name Obstacles to **User Layer 8**.

4.   We then go back to our cube entity and set its **Layers** property to `Obstacles`:

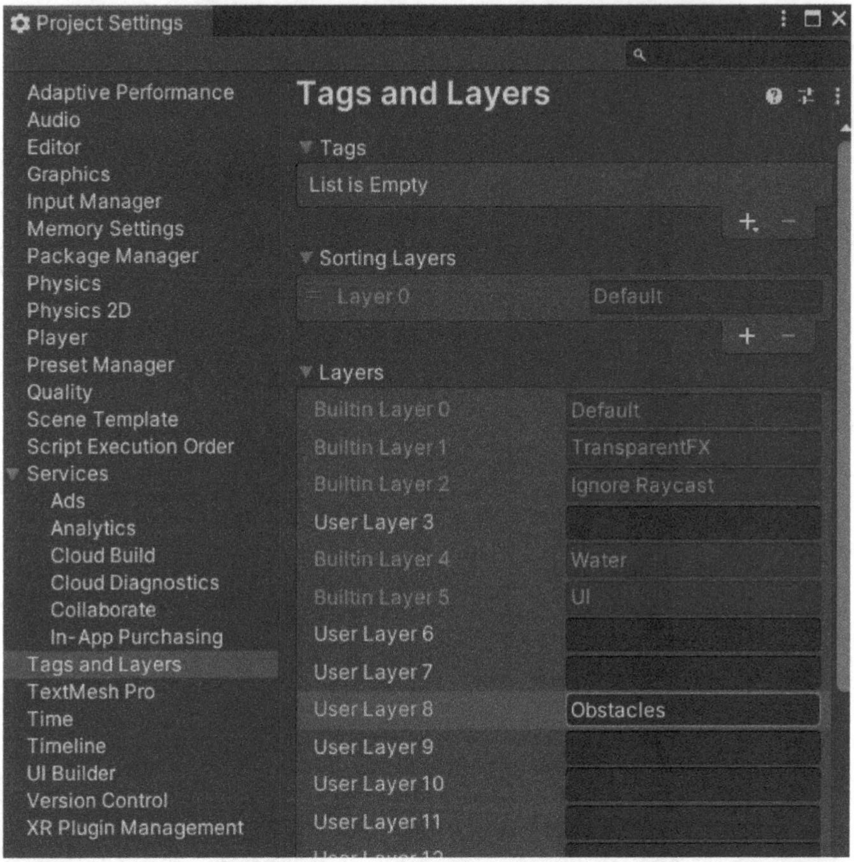

Figure 6.9 – Creating a new layer

5.   When we use raycasting to detect obstacles, we check for those entities, but only on this layer. This way, the physics system can ignore objects hit by a ray that are not an obstacle, such as bushes or vegetation:

Figure 6.10 – Assigning our new layer

6.   For larger projects, our game objects probably already have a layer assigned to them. As such, instead of changing the object's layer to **Obstacles**, we would instead make a list of layers for our cube entity to use when detecting obstacles. We will talk more about this in the next section.

> **Info**
>
> In games, we use layers to let cameras render only a part of the scene or have lights illuminate only a subset of the objects. However, layers can also be used by raycasting to ignore colliders selectively or to create collisions. You can learn more about this at `https://docs.unity3d.com/Manual/Layers.html`.

Obstacle avoidance

Now, it is time to code the script that makes the cube entity avoid the walls. As usual, we first initialize our entity script with the default properties. Here, we also draw GUI text in our OnGUI method. Let's take a look at the following code in the VehicleAvoidance. cs file:

```
using UnityEngine;

public class VehicleAvoidance : MonoBehaviour {
    public float vehicleRadius = 1.2f;
    public float speed = 10.0f;

    public float force = 50.0f;
    public float minimumDistToAvoid = 10.0f;
    public float targetReachedRadius = 3.0f;

    //Actual speed of the vehicle
    private float curSpeed;
    private Vector3 targetPoint;

    // Use this for initialization
    void Start() {
        targetPoint = Vector3.zero;
    }

    void OnGUI() {
        GUILayout.Label("Click anywhere to move the vehicle
                         to the clicked point");
    }
```

Then, in the `Update` method, we update the Agent entity's position and rotation based on the direction vector returned by the `AvoidObstacles` method:

```
void Update() {
    //Vehicle move by mouse click
    var ray = Camera.main.ScreenPointToRay(
      Input.mousePosition);

    if (Input.GetMouseButtonDown(0) &&
        Physics.Raycast(ray, out var hit, 100.0f)) {
        targetPoint = hit.point;
    }

    //Directional vector to the target position
    Vector3 dir = (targetPoint - transform.position);
    dir.Normalize();

    //Apply obstacle avoidance
    AvoidObstacles(ref dir);

        . . . .
}
```

The first thing we do in the `Update` method is to retrieve the position of the mouse-click. Then, we use this position to determine the desired target position of our character. To get the mouse-click position, we shoot a ray from the camera in the direction it's facing. Then, we take the point where the ray hits the ground plane as the target position.

Once we get the target position, we can calculate the direction vector by subtracting the current position vector from the target position vector. Then, we call the `AvoidObstacles` method passing this direction to it:

```
public void AvoidObstacles(ref Vector3 dir) {
    //Only detect layer 8 (Obstacles)
    int layerMask = 1 << 8;

    //Check that the vehicle hit with the obstacles
    //within it's minimum distance to avoid
    if (Physics.SphereCast(transform.position,
```

```
            vehicleRadius, transform.forward, out var hit,
            minimumDistToAvoid, layerMask)) {
            //Get the normal of the hit point to calculate
            //the new direction
            Vector3 hitNormal = hit.normal;
            //Don't want to move in Y-Space
            hitNormal.y = 0.0f;

            //Get the new directional vector by adding
            //force to vehicle's current forward vector
            dir = transform.forward + hitNormal * force;
        }


    }
```

The `AvoidObstacles` method is also quite simple. Note that we use another very useful Unity physics utility: a **SphereCast**. A SphereCast is similar to the Raycast but, instead of detecting a collider by firing a dimensionless ray, it fires a chunky sphere. In practice, a SphereCast gives width to the Raycast ray.

Why is this important? Because our character is not dimensionless. We want to be sure that the entire body of the character can avoid the collision.

Another thing to note is that the SphereCast interacts selectively with the **Obstacles** layer we specified at **User Layer 8** in the Unity3D **Tag Manager**. The `SphereCast` method accepts a layer mask parameter to determine which layers to ignore and consider during raycasting. Now, if you look at how many layers you can specify in **Tag Manager**, you'll find a total of 32 layers.

Therefore, Unity3D uses a 32-bit integer number to represent this layer mask parameter. For example, the following would represent a zero in 32 bits:

```
0000 0000 0000 0000 0000 0000 0000 0000
```

By default, Unity3D uses the first eight layers as built-in layers. So, when you use a Raycast or a SphereCast without using a layer mask parameter, it detects every object in those eight layers. We can represent this interaction mask with a bitmask, as follows:

```
0000 0000 0000 0000 0000 0000 1111 1111
```

In this demo, we set the **Obstacles** layer as layer 8 (9th index). Because we only want to detect obstacles in this layer, we want to set up the bitmask in the following way:

```
0000 0000 0000 0000 0000 0001 0000 0000
```

The easiest way to set up this bitmask is by using the bit shift operators. We only need to place the on bit, 1, at the 9th index, which means we can just move that bit eight places to the left. So, we use the left shift operator to move the bit eight places to the left, as shown in the following code:

```
int layerMask = 1<<8;
```

If we wanted to use multiple layer masks, say, layer 8 and layer 9, an easy way would be to use the bitwise **OR** operator, as follows:

```
int layerMask = (1<<8) | (1<<9);
```

> **Info**
>
> You can also find a good discussion on using layer masks on Unity3D's online resources. The question and answer site can be found at `http://answers.unity3d.com/questions/8715/how-do-i-use-layermasks.html`.

Once we have the layer mask, we call the `Physics.SphereCast` method from the current entity's position and in the forward direction. We use a sphere of radius `vehicleRadius` (make sure that is big enough to contain the cubic vehicle in its entirety) and a detection distance defined by the `minimumDistToAvoid` variable. In fact, we want to detect only the objects that are close enough to affect our movement.

Then, we take the normal vector of the hit ray, multiply it with the force vector, and add it to the current direction of the entity to get the new resultant direction vector, which we return from this method:

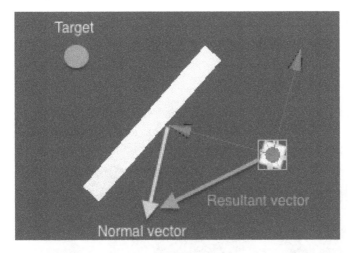

Figure 6.11 – How our cube entity avoids a wall

Then, in the Update method, we use this new direction to rotate the AI entity and update the position according to the speed value:

```
void Update () {

    //...

    //Don't move the vehicle when the target point is
    //reached
    if (Vector3.Distance(targetPoint,
        transform.position) < targetReachedRadius)
        return;

    //Assign the speed with delta time
    curSpeed = speed * Time.deltaTime;

    //Rotate the vehicle to its target directional
    //vector
    var rot = Quaternion.LookRotation(dir);
    transform.rotation =
        Quaternion.Slerp(transform.rotation, rot, 5.0f *
                        Time.deltaTime);

    //Move the vehicle towards
```

```
        transform.position += transform.forward * curSpeed;
        transform.position = new Vector3(
          transform.position.x, 0, transform.position.z);
    }
```

Now, we only need to attach this new script to the Vehicle object (this can be a simple cube as in the previous example). Remember that this new script needs to replace the `VehicleFollowing` script we implemented in the previous section.

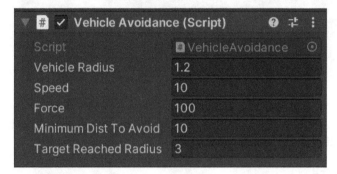

Figure 6.12 – Properties of our Vehicle Avoidance script

If everything is correct, you should be able to see the vehicle navigate across the plane around the obstacles without any trouble. As usual, play with the Inspector parameters to tweak the vehicle behavior.

Summary

In this chapter, we set up two scenes and studied how to build path-following agents with obstacle avoidance behavior. We learned about the Unity3D layer feature and how to use Raycasts and SphereCasts against a particular layer selectively. Although these examples were simple, we can apply these simple techniques to various scenarios. For instance, we can set up a path along a road. We can easily set up a decent traffic simulation using some vehicle models combined with obstacle avoidance behavior. Alternatively, you could just replace them with biped characters and build a crowd simulation. You can also combine them with some finite state machines to add more behaviors and make them more intelligent.

The simple obstacle avoidance behavior that we implemented in this chapter doesn't consider the optimal path to reach the target position. Instead, it just goes straight to that target, and only if an obstacle is seen within a certain distance does it try to avoid it. For this reason, it's supposed to be used among moving or dynamic objects and obstacles.

In the following chapter, we'll study how to implement a pathfinding algorithm, called **A***, to determine the optimal path before moving, while still avoiding static obstacles.

7
A* Pathfinding

In this chapter, we will implement the **A* algorithm** in Unity3D using C#. The A*
pathfinding algorithm is widely used in games and interactive applications because of
its simplicity and effectiveness. We talked about this algorithm previously in *Chapter 1,
Introduction to AI*. However, here, we'll review the algorithm again, this time from an
implementation perspective.

In this chapter, we will look at the following topics:

- Revisiting the A* algorithm
- Implementing the A* algorithm
- Setting up the scene
- Testing the pathfinder

Technical requirements

For this chapter, you just need Unity3D 2022. You can find the example project described
in this chapter in the `Chapter 7` folder in the book repository: `https://github.
com/PacktPublishing/Unity-Artificial-Intelligence-Programming-
Fifth-Edition/tree/main/Chapter07`.

Revisiting the A* algorithm

Let's review the A* algorithm before we proceed to implement it in the next section. The foundation of any pathfinding algorithm is a representation of the world. Pathfinding algorithms cannot search over the noisy structure of polygons in the game map; instead, we need to provide them with a simplified version of the world. Using this simplified structure, we can identify the locations that an agent can traverse, as well as the inaccessible ones.

There are many ways of doing this; however, for this example, we use one of the most straightforward solutions: a 2D grid. Therefore, we implement the `GridManager` class to convert the "real" map into a 2D tile representation. The `GridManager` class keeps a list of `Node` objects representing a single tile in the 2D grid. First, of course, we need to implement the `Node` class too: this class stores node information such as its position, whether it's a traversable node or an obstacle, the cost to pass through, and the cost to reach the target node.

Once we have a world representation, we implement an `AStar` class for the actual A* pathfinding algorithm. The class is elementary; the `FindPath` method includes all the work. The class has two variables to keep track of the already visited nodes and the nodes that will be explored. We call these variables the **closed list** and **open list**, respectively. We implement the open list with a `PriorityQueue` class because we want to get `Node` with the lowest score as fast as possible.

Instead, the closed list wants a data structure that allows us to efficiently check whether it contains a specific `Node`: usually, a data structure called a **set** is a good choice.

Finally, the A* pseudocode is outlined here:

1. First, the algorithm takes the starting node and puts it in the open list.
2. As long as the open list is not empty, the algorithm proceeds to perform the following steps.
3. It picks the first node from the open list and defines it as the current node (of course, we are assuming that we are using PriorityQueues for the open list).

4. Then, it gets the neighboring nodes of this current node, excluding obstacle types (such as a wall or canyon that can't be passed through). This step is usually called expansion.

5. For each neighbor node in step 4, it checks whether it is already in the closed list. If not, it calculates the total cost (F) for this neighbor node using the following formula:

$$F = G + H$$

Here, G is the total cost from the starting node to this node (usually computed by adding the cost of moving from parent to neighbor to the G value of the parent node), and H is the estimated total cost from this node to the final target node. We will go over the problem of estimating the cost in later sections.

6. The algorithm stores that cost data in the neighbor node object, and it assigns the current node as the neighbor's parent node. Later, we use this parent node data to trace back the starting node from the end node, thus reconstructing the actual path.

7. It puts this neighbor node in the open list. The open list is a priority queue ordered by the F value; therefore, the first node in the open list is always the one with the lowest F value.

8. If there are no more neighbor nodes to process, the algorithm puts the current node in the closed list and removes it from the open list.

9. The algorithm goes back to step 2.

Once you have completed this algorithm, if there's an obstacle-free path to reach the target node from the start node, your current node is precisely at the target node position. Otherwise, this means that there's no available path to the target node from the current node position.

When we get a valid path, we have to trace back from the current node using the parent pointer until we reach the start node again. This procedure gives us a path listing all the nodes we chose during our pathfinding process, ordered from the target node to the start node. As a final step, we just reverse this path list and get the path in the proper order.

Next, we will implement A* in Unity3D using C#. So, let's get started.

Implementing the A* algorithm

First, we implement the basic classes that we introduced before, such as the Node class, the GridManager class, and the PriorityQueue class. Then, we use them in the main AStar class.

Node

The Node class represents each tile object in the 2D grid. Its code is shown in the Node.cs file:

```
using UnityEngine;
using System;

public class Node {
    public float costSoFar;
    public float fScore;
    public bool isObstacle;
    public Node parent;
    public Vector3 position;


    public Node(Vector3 pos) {
        fScore = 0.0f;
        costSoFar = 0.0f;
        isObstacle = false;
        parent = null;
        position = pos;
    }

    public void MarkAsObstacle() {
        isObstacle = true;
    }
```

The Node class stores every valuable property we need for finding a path. We are talking about properties such as the cost from the starting point (`costSoFar`), the total estimated cost from start to end (`fScore`), a flag to mark whether it is an obstacle, its positions, and its parent node. `costSoFar` is *G*, which is the movement cost value from the starting node to this node so far, and `fScore` is obviously *F*, which is the total estimated cost from the start to the target node. We also have two simple constructor methods and a wrapper method to set, depending on whether this node is an obstacle or not. Then, we implement the `Equals` and `GetHashCode` methods, as shown in the following code:

```
public override bool Equals(object obj) {
    return obj is Node node &&
            position.Equals(node.position);
}

public override int GetHashCode() {
    return HashCode.Combine(position);
}
}
```

These methods are important. In fact, even if the Node class has multiple attributes, two nodes that represent the same position should be considered equal as far as the search algorithm is concerned. The way to do that is to override the default `Equals` and `GetHashCode` methods, as in the preceding example.

PriorityQueue

A **priority queue** is an ordered data structure designed so that the first element (the head) of the list is always the smallest or largest element (depending on the implementation). This data structure is the most efficient way to handle the nodes in the open list because, as we will see later, we need to quickly retrieve the node with the lowest *F* value.

Unfortunately, there is no easy out-of-the-box way to have a suitable priority queue (at least, until Unity supports .NET 6). The code we will use for this is shown in the following `NodePriorityQueue.cs` class:

```
using System.Collections.Generic;
using System.Linq;
```

```
public class NodePriorityQueue {
    private readonly List<Node> nodes = new();

    public int Length {
        get { return nodes.Count; }
    }

    public bool Contains(Node node) {
        return nodes.Contains(node);
    }

    public Node Dequeue() {
        if (nodes.Count > 0) {
            var result = nodes[0];
            nodes.RemoveAt(0);
            return result;
        }
        return null;
    }

    public void Enqueue(Node node) {
        if (nodes.Contains(node)) {
            var oldNode = nodes.First(n => n.Equals(node));
            if (oldNode.fScore <= node.fScore) {
                return;
            } else {
                nodes.Remove(oldNode);
            }
        }
        nodes.Add(node);
        nodes.Sort((n1, n2) => n1.fScore < n2.fScore ? -1 :
                1);
    }

}
```

This implementation is not particularly efficient because it relies on the `Sort` method to reorder the internal list of nodes after each insertion. This means that inserting a node becomes increasingly costly the more nodes we have in the queue. If you need better performance, you can find many priority queue implementations designed for A* and search algorithms (such as the one you can find at `https://github.com/BlueRaja/High-Speed-Priority-Queue-for-C-Sharp`).

For now, though, our small `NodePriorityQueue` class will do its job nicely. The class is self-explanatory. The only thing you need to pay attention to is the `Enqueue` method. Before adding a new node, we need to check whether there is already a node with the same position but a lower F-score. If there is, we do nothing (we already have a *better* node in the queue). If not, this means that the new node we are adding is better than the old one. Therefore, we can remove the old one to ensure that we only have the best node possible for each position.

The GridManager class

The `GridManager` class handles the 2D grid representation for the world map. We keep it as a singleton instance of the `GridManager` class, as we only need one object to represent the map. A singleton is a programming pattern that restricts the instantiation of a class to one object and, therefore, it makes the instance easily accessible from any point of the application. The code for setting up `GridManager` is shown in the `GridManager.cs` file.

1. The first part of the class implements the **singleton pattern**. We look for the `GridManager` object in the scene and, if we find it, we store it in the `staticInstance` static variable:

```
using UnityEngine;
using System.Collections.Generic;

public class GridManager : MonoBehaviour {
    private static GridManager staticInstance = null;

    public static GridManager instance {
        get {
            if (staticInstance == null) {
                staticInstance = FindObjectOfType(
                    typeof(GridManager)) as GridManager;
                if (staticInstance == null)
```

```
                Debug.Log("Could not locate an
                GridManager object. \n You have
                to have exactly one GridManager
                in the scene.");
        }
        return staticInstance;
    }
}


// Ensure that the instance is destroyed when the
// game is stopped in the editor.
void OnApplicationQuit() {
    staticInstance = null;
}
```

2. Then, we declare all the variables that we need to represent our map. numOfRows
    and numOfColumns store the number of rows and columns of the grid.
    gridCellSize represents the size of each grid. obstacleEpsilon is the
    margin for the system we will use to detect obstacles (more on that later).

3. Then we have two Boolean variables to enable or disable the debug visualization of
    the grid and obstacles. Finally, we have a grid of nodes representing the map itself.
    We also add two properties to get the grid's origin in world coordinates (Origin)
    and the cost of moving from one tile to the other (StepCost). The final product is
    shown in the following code:

```
public int numOfRows;
public int numOfColumns;
public float gridCellSize;
public float obstacleEpsilon = 0.2f;
public bool showGrid = true;
public bool showObstacleBlocks = true;


public Node[,] nodes { get; set; }


public Vector3 Origin {
    get { return transform.position; }
```

```
    }

    public float StepCost {
        get { return gridCellSize; }
    }
```

4. Now we need to build the grid. For this, we use the `ComputeGrid` method that we call on `Awake`. The code is shown here:

```
void Awake() {
    ComputeGrid();
}


void ComputeGrid() {
    //Initialise the nodes
    nodes = new Node[numOfColumns, numOfRows];

    for (int i = 0; i < numOfColumns; i++) {
        for (int j = 0; j < numOfRows; j++) {
            Vector3 cellPos =
                GetGridCellCenter(i,j);
            Node node = new(cellPos);


            var collisions =
                Physics.OverlapSphere(cellPos,
                gridCellSize / 2 - obstacleEpsilon,
                1 << LayerMask.NameToLayer(
                "Obstacles"));
            if (collisions.Length != 0) {
                node.MarkAsObstacle();
            }
            nodes[i, j] = node;
        }
    }
}
```

5. The `ComputeGrid` function follows a simple algorithm. First, we just initialize the `nodes` grid. Then we start iterating over each square of the grid (represented by the coordinates i and j). For each square, we do as follows:

    I.   First, we create a new node positioned at the center of the square (in world coordinates).

    II. Then, we check whether that square is occupied by an obstacle. We do this by using the `OverlapSphere` function. This `Physics` function returns all the colliders inside or intersecting the sphere defined in the parameters. In our case, we center the sphere at the center of the grid's cell (`cellPos`) and we define the sphere's radius as a bit less than the grid cell size. Note that we are only interested in colliders in the `Obstacles` layer, therefore we need to add the appropriate layer mask.

    III. If the `OverlapSphere` function returns anything, this means that we have an obstacle inside the cell and, therefore, we define the entire cell as an obstacle.

`GridManager` also has several helper methods to traverse the grid and get the grid cell data. We show some of them in the following list, with a brief description of what they do. The implementation is simple:

1. The `GetGridCellCenter` method returns the position of the grid cell in world coordinates from the cell coordinates, as shown in the following code:

```
public Vector3 GetGridCellCenter(int col, int row)
{
    Vector3 cellPosition =
      GetGridCellPosition(col, row);
    cellPosition.x += gridCellSize / 2.0f;
    cellPosition.z += gridCellSize / 2.0f;

    return cellPosition;
}

public Vector3 GetGridCellPosition(int col, int
  row) {
    float xPosInGrid = col * gridCellSize;
    float zPosInGrid = row * gridCellSize;

    return Origin + new Vector3(xPosInGrid, 0.0f,
```

```
        zPosInGrid);
    }
```

2. The `IsInBounds` method checks whether a certain position in the game falls inside the grid:

```
public bool IsInBounds(Vector3 pos) {
    float width = numOfColumns * gridCellSize;
    float height = numOfRows * gridCellSize;

    return (pos.x >= Origin.x && pos.x <= Origin.x +
        width && pos.x <= Origin.z + height && pos.z >=
        Origin.z);
}
```

3. The `IsTraversable` method checks whether a grid coordinate is traversable (that is, it is not an obstacle):

```
public bool IsTraversable(int col, int row) {
    return col >= 0 && row >= 0 && col <
        numOfColumns && row < numOfRows &&
        !nodes[col, row].isObstacle;
}
```

4. Another important method is `GetNeighbours`, which is used by the `AStar` class to retrieve the neighboring nodes of a particular node. This is done by obtaining the grid coordinate of the node and then checking whether the four neighbors' coordinates (up, down, left, and right) are traversable:

```
public List<Node> GetNeighbours(Node node) {
    List<Node> result = new();
    var (column, row) =
        GetGridCoordinates(node.position);

    if (IsTraversable(column - 1, row)) {
        result.Add(nodes[column - 1, row]);
    }
    if (IsTraversable(column + 1, row)) {
        result.Add(nodes[column + 1, row]);
    }
```

```
        if (IsTraversable(column, row - 1)) {
            result.Add(nodes[column, row - 1]);
        }
        if (IsTraversable(column, row + 1)) {
            result.Add(nodes[column, row + 1]);
        }
        return result;
}
```

5. Finally, we have debug aid methods used to visualize the grid and obstacle blocks:

```
void OnDrawGizmos() {
    if (showGrid) {
        DebugDrawGrid(Color.blue);
    }

    //Grid Start Position
    Gizmos.DrawSphere(Origin, 0.5f);

    if (nodes == null) return;

    //Draw Obstacle obstruction
    if (showObstacleBlocks) {
        Vector3 cellSize = new Vector3(
            gridCellSize, 1.0f, gridCellSize);
        Gizmos.color = Color.red;
        for (int i = 0; i < numOfColumns; i++) {
            for (int j = 0; j < numOfRows; j++) {
                if (nodes != null && nodes[i,
                    j].isObstacle) {
                    Gizmos.DrawCube(
                        GetGridCellCenter(i,j),
                        cellSize);
                }
            }
        }
    }
}
```

```
    }

    public void DebugDrawGrid(Color color) {
        float width = (numOfColumns * gridCellSize);
        float height = (numOfRows * gridCellSize);

        // Draw the horizontal grid lines
        for (int i = 0; i < numOfRows + 1; i++) {
            Vector3 startPos = Origin + i *
                gridCellSize * new Vector3(0.0f, 0.0f,
                                                1.0f);
            Vector3 endPos = startPos + width * new
                Vector3(1.0f, 0.0f, 0.0f);
            Debug.DrawLine(startPos, endPos, color);
        }

        // Draw the vertial grid lines
        for (int i = 0; i < numOfColumns + 1; i++) {
            Vector3 startPos = Origin + i *
                gridCellSize * new Vector3(1.0f, 0.0f,
                                                0.0f);
            Vector3 endPos = startPos + height * new
                Vector3(0.0f, 0.0f, 1.0f);
            Debug.DrawLine(startPos, endPos, color);
        }
    }
```

Gizmos can be used to draw visual debugging and setup aids inside the editor scene view. OnDrawGizmos is called every frame by the engine. So, if the debug flags, showGrid and showObstacleBlocks, are checked, we just draw the grid with lines and the obstacle cube objects with cubes. We won't go through the DebugDrawGrid method, as it's pretty simple.

Info

You can learn more about gizmos in the following Unity3D reference documentation: https://docs.unity3d.com/ScriptReference/Gizmos.html.

The AStar class

The `AStar` class implements the pathfinding algorithm using the classes we have implemented so far. If you want a quick review of the A* algorithm, see the *Revisiting the A* algorithm* section earlier in this chapter. The steps for the implementation of `AStar` are as follows:

1. We start by implementing a method called `HeuristicEstimateCost` to calculate the cost between the two nodes. The calculation is simple. We just find the direction vector between the two by subtracting one position vector from another. The magnitude of this resultant vector gives the straight-line distance from the current node to the target node:

```
using UnityEngine;
using System.Collections.Generic;

public class AStar {
    private float HeuristicEstimateCost(Node curNode,
        Node goalNode) {
        return (curNode.position -
                goalNode.position).magnitude;
    }
```

> **Info**
>
> In theory, you can replace this function with any function, returning the distance between `curNode` and `goalNode`. However, for A* to return the shortest possible path, this function must be admissible. In short, an admissible heuristic function is a function that never overestimates the actual "real world" cost between `curNode` and `goalNode`. As an exercise, you can easily verify that the function we use in this demo is admissible. For more information on the math behind heuristic functions, you can visit `https://theory.stanford.edu/~amitp/GameProgramming/Heuristics.html`.

2. Then, we have the main A* algorithm in the `FindPath` method. In the following snippet, we initialize the open and closed lists. Starting with the start node, we put it in our open list. Then, we start processing our open list:

```
public List<Node> FindPath(Node start, Node goal) {
    //Start Finding the path
    NodePriorityQueue openList =
```

```
                    new NodePriorityQueue();
            openList.Enqueue(start);
            start.costSoFar = 0.0f;
            start.fScore = HeuristicEstimateCost(start,
                                                    goal);

            HashSet<Node> closedList = new();
            Node node = null;
```

3. Then, we proceed with the main algorithm loop:

```
            while (openList.Length != 0) {
                node = openList.Dequeue();

                if (node.position == goal.position) {
                    return CalculatePath(node);
                }

                var neighbours =
                    GridManager.instance.GetNeighbours(
                    node);

                foreach (Node neighbourNode in neighbours)
                {
                    if (!closedList.Contains(
                        neighbourNode)) {
                        float totalCost = node.costSoFar +
                            GridManager.instance.StepCost;
                        float heuristicValue =
                            HeuristicEstimateCost(
                            neighbourNode, goal);

                        //Assign neighbour node properties
                        neighbourNode.costSoFar =
                            totalCost;
                        neighbourNode.parent = node;
```

```
                        neighbourNode.fScore =
                    totalCost + heuristicValue;


                    //Add the neighbour node to the
                    //queue
                    if (!closedList.Contains(
                        neighbourNode)) {
                            openList.Enqueue(
                                neighbourNode);
                    }


                }
            }
        closedList.Add(node);

    }
```

I.   The preceding code implementation strictly follows the algorithm that we have discussed previously, so you can refer back to it if something is not clear:

II. Get the first node from our `openList`. Remember, `openList` is always sorted in increasing order. Therefore, the first node is always the node with the lowest *F* value.

III. Check whether the current node is already at the target node. If so, exit the `while` loop and build the path array.

IV. Create an array list to store the neighboring nodes of the current node being processed. Then, use the `GetNeighbours` method to retrieve the neighbors from the grid.

V.   For every node in the array of neighbors, we check whether it's already in `closedList`. If not, we calculate the cost values, update the node properties with the new cost values and the parent node data, and put it in `openList`.

VI. Push the current node to `closedList` and remove it from `openList`.

VII. Go back to *step I*.

4. If there are no more nodes in `openList`, the current node should be at the target node if there's a valid path available:

```
        //If finished looping and cannot find the goal
        //then return null
        if (node.position != goal.position) {
```

```
                    Debug.LogError("Goal Not Found");
                    return null;
            }

            //Calculate the path based on the final node
            return CalculatePath(node);
```

5. Finally, we call the `CalculatePath` method with the current node parameter:

```
        private List<Node> CalculatePath(Node node) {
            List<Node> list = new();
            while (node != null) {
                list.Add(node);
                node = node.parent;
            }
            list.Reverse();
            return list;
        }
    }
```

6. The `CalculatePath` method traces through each node's parent `node` object and builds an array list. Since we want a path array from the start node to the target node, we just call the `Reverse` method.

Now, we'll write a test script to test this and set up a demo scene.

The TestCode class

The `TestCode` class uses the `AStar` class to find the path from the start node to the target node, as shown in the following code from the `TestCode.cs` file:

```
using UnityEngine;
using System.Collections;

public class TestCode : MonoBehaviour {
    private Transform startPos, endPos;
    public Node startNode { get; set; }
    public Node goalNode { get; set; }
    public List<Node> pathArray;
```

```
        GameObject objStartCube, objEndCube;
        private float elapsedTime = 0.0f;
        //Interval time between pathfinding
        public float intervalTime = 1.0f;
```

In the preceding snippet, we first set up the variables that we need to reference. The pathArray variable stores the nodes array that's returned from the AStar FindPath method.

In the following code block, we use the Start method to look for objects with the tags Start and End and initialize pathArray. We are trying to find a new path at every interval, specified by the intervalTime property, in case the positions of the start and end nodes have changed. Finally, we call the FindPath method:

```
    void Start () {
        objStartCube =
          GameObject.FindGameObjectWithTag("Start");
        objEndCube =
          GameObject.FindGameObjectWithTag("End");


        pathArray = new List<Node>();
        FindPath();
    }


    void Update () {
        elapsedTime += Time.deltaTime;
        if (elapsedTime >= intervalTime) {
            elapsedTime = 0.0f;
            FindPath();
        }
    }
```

Since we implemented our pathfinding algorithm in the AStar class, finding a path is much simpler. In the following snippet, we first take the positions of the start and end game objects. Then, we create new Node objects using the GetGridIndex helper methods in GridManager to calculate their respective row and column index positions inside the grid.

After that, we call the `AStar.FindPath` method with the start node and target node, storing the returned array list in the local `pathArray` property. Finally, we implement the `OnDrawGizmos` method to draw and visualize the resulting path:

```
void FindPath() {
        startPos = objStartCube.transform;
        endPos = objEndCube.transform;

        //Assign StartNode and Goal Node
        var (startColumn, startRow) =
          GridManager.instance.GetGridCoordinates(
          startPos.position);
        var (goalColumn, goalRow) =
          GridManager.instance.GetGridCoordinates(
          endPos.position);
        startNode = new Node(
          GridManager.instance.GetGridCellCenter(
          startColumn, startRow));
        goalNode = new Node(
          GridManager.instance.GetGridCellCenter(
          goalColumn, goalRow));

        pathArray =
          new AStar().FindPath(startNode, goalNode);
}
```

We look through our `pathArray` and use the `Debug.DrawLine` method to draw the lines, connecting the nodes in `pathArray`:

```
    void OnDrawGizmos() {
        if (pathArray == null)
            return;

        if (pathArray.Count > 0) {
            int index = 1;
            foreach (Node node in pathArray) {
                if (index < pathArray.Count) {
                    Node nextNode = pathArray[index];
```

```
                      Debug.DrawLine(node.position,
                          nextNode.position, Color.green);
                      index++;
                  }
              };
          }
      }
  }
```

When we run and test our program, we should see a green line connecting the nodes from start to end.

Setting up the scene

We are going to set up a scene that looks like the following screenshot:

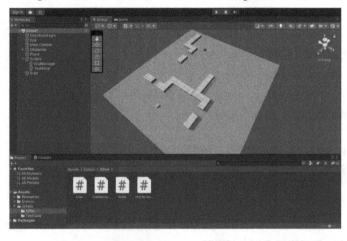

Figure 7.1 – Our sample test scene with obstacles

Let's follow a step-by-step procedure to do this:

1. We create a directional light, the start and end game object, a few obstacle objects, a plane entity to be used as ground, and two empty game objects in which we put the GridManager and TestAStar scripts. After this step, our scene hierarchy should be like this:

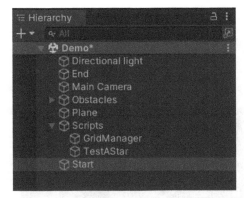

Figure 7.2 – The demo scene hierarchy

2. We create a bunch of cube entities and add them to the **Obstacles** layer. GridManager looks for objects with this tag when it creates the grid world representation:

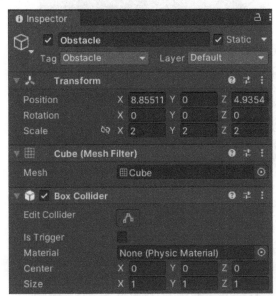

Figure 7.3 – The Obstacle nodes seen in the Inspector

3. We then create a cube entity and tag it as **Start**:

Figure 7.4 – The Start node seen in the Inspector

4. Then, we create another cube entity and tag it as **End**:

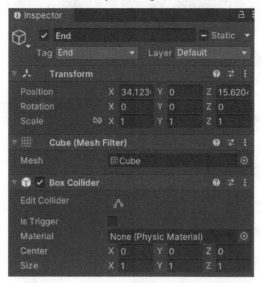

Figure 7.5 – The End node seen in the Inspector

5. We create an empty game object, and we attach the GridManager script to it. We also set the name to GridManager because we use this name to look for the GridManager object from inside the other scripts.

6. Then, we set up the number of rows and columns of the grid and the size of each tile.

Figure 7.6 – GridManager script

Testing the pathfinder

Once we hit the **Play** button, we should see the A* pathfinding algorithm in action. By default, once you play the scene, Unity3D switches to the **Game** view. However, since our pathfinding visualization code draws in the debug editor view, to see the found path, you need to switch back to the **Scene** view or enable **Gizmos** visualization:

Figure 7.7 – The first path found by the algorithm

Now, try to move the start or end node around in the scene using the editor's movement gizmo (not in the **Game** view, but the **Scene** view):

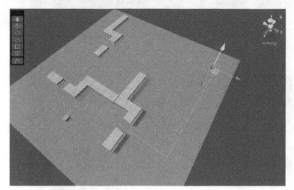

Figure 7.8 – A second path found by the algorithm

You should see that the path is updated dynamically in real time. On the other hand, if there is no available path, you get an error message in the console window instead.

Summary

In this chapter, we learned how to implement the A* pathfinding algorithm in Unity3D. First, we implemented our own A* pathfinding class, grid representation class, priority queue class, and node class. Finally, we used debug draw functionalities to visualize the grid and path information.

In later chapters, we will see that thanks to Unity3D's **NavMesh** and **NavAgent** features, it may not be necessary for you to implement a custom pathfinding algorithm on your own.

Nonetheless, understanding a basic pathfinding algorithm gives you a better foundation for getting to grips with many other advanced pathfinding techniques.

In the next chapter, we will extend the idea behind the A* algorithm to a more complex world representation: navigation meshes.

8
Navigation Mesh

As we saw in *Chapter 7, A* Pathfinding*, the most critical decision in pathfinding is how to represent the scene's geometry. The AI agents need to know where the obstacles are, and it is our job as AI designers to provide the best representation we can to the pathfinding algorithm. Previously, we created a custom representation by dividing the map into a 2D grid, and then we implemented a custom pathfinding algorithm by implementing A* using that representation. But wouldn't it be awesome if Unity could do all that for us?

Fortunately, Unity can do this using **Navigation Meshes (NavMeshes)**. While in the previous 2D representation, we divided the world into perfect squares, with NavMeshes, we will divide the world using arbitrary convex polygons. This representation has two exciting advantages: first, every polygon can be different, and therefore we can use a small number of big polygons for vast open areas and many smaller polygons for very crowded spaces; second, we do not need to lock the Agent on a grid anymore, and so the pathfinding produces more natural paths.

This chapter will explain how we can use Unity's built-in NavMesh generator to make pathfinding for AI agents much easier and more performant. Some years ago, NavMeshes were an exclusive Unity Pro feature. Fortunately, this is not true anymore; NavMeshes are available in the free version of Unity for everyone!

In this chapter, we will cover the following topics:

- Setting up the map
- Building the scene with slopes

- Creating navigation areas

- An overview of Off Mesh Links

Technical requirements

For this chapter, you just need Unity3D 2022. You can find the example project described in this chapter in the Chapter 8 folder in the book repository: https://github. com/PacktPublishing/Unity-Artificial-Intelligence-Programming-Fifth-Edition/tree/main/Chapter08.

Setting up the map

To get started, let's build a simple scene, as shown in the following screenshot. This is the first scene in the example project and is called NavMesh01-Simple.scene. You can use a plane as the ground object and several cube entities as the wall objects:

Figure 8.1 – An image of the NavMesh01-Simple scene, a plane with obstacles

In the following subsections, we will set up the walls as obstacles, bake the NavMesh, and configure the tanks.

Navigation static

Once we add the floor and the obstacles, it is essential to mark them with the **Navigation Static** tag so that the NavMesh generator knows that they need to be taken into account during the baking process. To do this, select all of the objects, click on the **Static** button, and choose **Navigation Static**, as shown in the following screenshot:

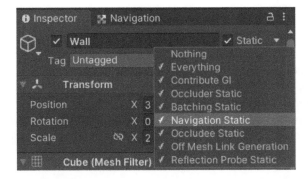

Figure 8.2 – The Navigation Static property

Baking the NavMesh

Now that we have completed the scene, let's bake the NavMesh. To do that, follow these steps:

1. Navigate to **Window | AI | Navigation**, and you should be able to see this window:

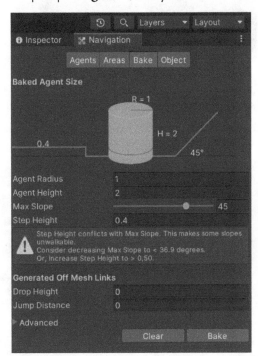

Figure 8.3 – Navigation window

> **Info**
>
> All the properties in the **Navigation** window are pretty self-explanatory: **Agent Radius** and **Agent Height** represent the size of the virtual agent used by Unity to bake the NavMesh, **Max Slope** is the value in degrees of the sharpest incline the character can walk up, and so on. If we have multiple AI agents, we should bake the NavMesh using the radius and height of the *smallest* AI character. For more information, you can check out the following Unity reference documentation: `https://docs.unity3d.com/Manual/Navigation.html`.

2. Select the plane and, in the **Object** tab, set its area to **Walkable**.

Figure 8.4 – The Object section of the Navigation panel

3. Leave everything else with the default values and click on **Bake**.

4. You should see a progress bar baking the NavMesh for your scene, and after a while, you should see the NavMesh in your scene, as shown in the following screenshot:

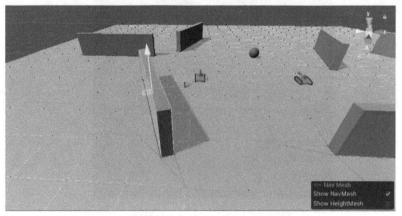

Figure 8.5 – The baking of a NavMesh

NavMesh agent

At this point, we have completed the super-simple scene setup. Now, let's add some AI agents to see if it works:

1. As a character, we use our trustworthy tank model. However, do not worry if you're working in a different scene and have a different model. Everything works the same way independently of the model.

Figure 8.6 – Tank entity

2. Add the **Nav Mesh Agent** component to our tank entity. This component makes pathfinding easy. We do not need to implement pathfinding algorithms such as A* anymore. Instead, we only need to set the destination property of the component at runtime, and the component will compute the path using Unity's internal pathfinding algorithm.

3.   Navigate to **Component | Navigation | Nav Mesh Agent** to add this component:

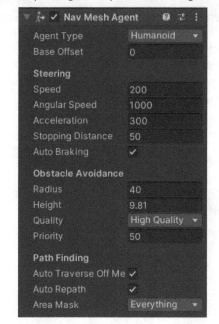

Figure 8.7 – Nav Mesh Agent properties

Info

You can find the official Unity reference for the **Nav Mesh Agent** at `https://docs.unity3d.com/Manual/class-NavMeshAgent.html`.

One property to note is the **Area Mask** property. It specifies the NavMesh layers that this NavMesh agent can walk on. We will talk about navigation layers in the *Baking navigation areas* section.

Updating an agent's destinations

Now that we have set up our AI agent, we need a way to tell it where to go and update the destination of the tank to the mouse click position.

So, let's add a sphere entity, which we use as a marker object, and then attach the `Target.cs` script to an empty game object. Then, drag and drop this sphere entity onto this script's `targetMarker` transform property in the Inspector.

The Target.cs class

This script contains a simple class that does three things:

- Gets the mouse click position using a ray
- Updates the marker position
- Updates the destination property of all the NavMesh agents

The following lines show the Target class's code:

```
using UnityEngine;
using System.Collections;

public class Target : MonoBehaviour {
    private UnityEngine.AI.NavMeshAgent[] navAgents;
    public Transform targetMarker;
    public float verticalOffset = 10.0f;

    void Start() {
        navAgents = FindObjectsOfType(
            typeof(UnityEngine.AI.NavMeshAgent)) as
            UnityEngine.AI.NavMeshAgent[];
    }

    void UpdateTargets(Vector3 targetPosition) {
        foreach (UnityEngine.AI.NavMeshAgent agent in
                navAgents) {
            agent.destination = targetPosition;
        }
    }

    void Update() {
        // Get the point of the hit position when the mouse
        // is being clicked
        if(Input.GetMouseButtonDown(0)) {
            Ray ray = Camera.main.ScreenPointToRay(
                Input.mousePosition);
```

```
            if (Physics.Raycast(ray.origin, ray.direction,
                out var hitInfo)) {
                Vector3 targetPosition = hitInfo.point;
                UpdateTargets(targetPosition);
                targetMarker.position = targetPosition +
                    new Vector3(0, verticalOffset, 0);
            }
        }
    }
}
```

At the start of the game, we look for all the **NavMeshAgent** type entities in our game and store them in our referenced NavMeshAgent array (note that if you want to spawn new agents at runtime, you need to update the navAgents list). Then, whenever there's a mouse click event, we do a simple raycast to determine the first object colliding with the ray. If the beam hits an object, we update the position of our marker and update each NavMesh agent's destination by setting the destination property with the new position. We will be using this script throughout this chapter to tell the destination position for our AI agents.

Now, test the scene, and click on a point that you want your tanks to go to. The tanks should move as close as possible to that point while avoiding every static obstacle (in this case, the walls).

Setting up a scene with slopes

Let's build a scene with some slopes, like this:

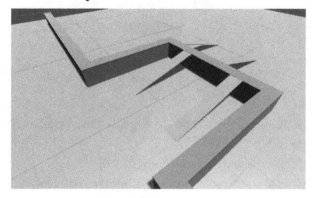

Figure 8.8 – Scene with slopes-NavMesh02-Slope.scene

One important thing to note is that the slopes and the wall should be in contact. If we want to use NavMeshes, objects need to be perfectly connected. Otherwise, there'll be gaps in the NavMesh, and the Agents will not be able to find the path anymore. There's a feature called **Off Mesh Link** generation to solve similar problems, but we will look at Off Mesh Links in the *Using Off Mesh Links* section later in this chapter. For now, let's concentrate on building the slope:

1. Make sure to connect the slope properly:

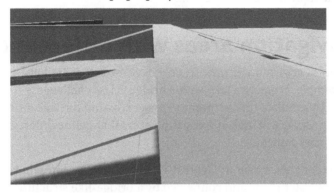

Figure 8.9 – A well-connected slope

2. We can adjust the **Max Slope** property in the Navigation window's **Bake** tab according to the level of slope in our scenes that we want to allow the Agents to travel. We'll use 45 degrees here. If your slopes are steeper than this, you can use a higher **Max Slope** value.

3. Bake the scene, and you should have generated a NavMesh, like this:

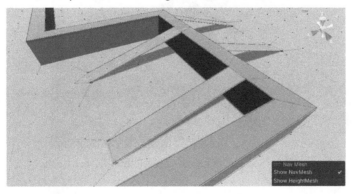

Figure 8.10 – The generated NavMesh

4. We will place some tanks with the **Nav Mesh Agent** component.

5. Create a new cube object and use it as the target reference position.

6. We will be using our previous `Target.cs` script to update the destination property of the AI agent.

7. Test run the scene, and you should see the AI agent crossing the slopes to reach the target.

Congratulation, you have implemented your first basic NavMesh-powered AI. Now, you can implement agents able to navigate over simple plains. What if we want more complex scenarios? That's the topic of the next section.

Baking navigation areas with different costs

In games with complex environments, we usually have areas that are harder to traverse than others. For example, crossing a lake with a bridge is less challenging than crossing it without a bridge. To simulate this, we want to make crossing the lake more costly than using a bridge. This section will look at navigation areas that define different layers with different navigation cost values.

For this, we build a scene, as shown in *Figure 8.11*. Three planes represent two ground planes separated by a water plane and connected by a bridge-like structure. As you can see, crossing over the water plane is the most direct way to traverse the lake; however, passing through the water costs more than using the bridge and, therefore, the pathfinding algorithm will prefer the bridge to the water:

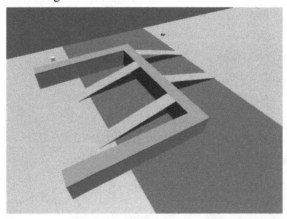

Figure 8.11 – Scene with layers – NavMesh03-Layers.scene

Let's follow a step-by-step procedure so that we can create a navigation area:

1. Go to the **Navigation** window and select the **Areas** section:

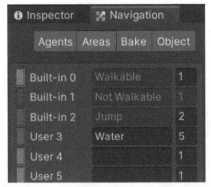

Figure 8.12 – The Areas section in the Navigation window

Unity comes with three default layers: **Default**, **Not Walkable**, and **Jump**, each with potentially different cost values.

2. Let's add a new layer called Water and give it a cost of 5.

3. Select the water plane.

4. Go to the **Navigation** window and, in the **Object** tab, set **Navigation Area** to **Water**:

Figure 8.13 – Water layer

5. Bake the NavMesh for the scene and run it to test it.

You should see that the AI agents now choose the slope rather than going through the plane marked as the water layer because it's more expensive to traverse the water. Try experimenting with placing the target object at different points on the water plane. You should see that the AI agents sometimes swim back to the shore and sometimes take the bridge rather than trying to swim across the water.

> **Info**
>
> You can find the official Unity documentation for **NavMesh Areas** at `https://docs.unity3d.com/Manual/nav-AreasAndCosts.html`.

Using Off Mesh Links to connect gaps between areas

Sometimes, there may be some gaps in the scene that can make the NavMeshes disconnected. For instance, the Agents do not find a path in our previous examples if we do not tightly connect the slopes to the walls, so we need to make it possible to jump over such gaps. In another example, we may want to set up points where our agents can jump off the wall onto the plane below. Unity has a feature called **Off Mesh Links** to connect such gaps. Off Mesh Links can be set up manually or can be automatically generated by Unity's NavMesh generator.

Here's the scene that we're going to build in this example. As you can see in *Figure 8.14*, there's a small gap between the two planes.

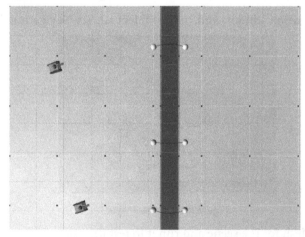

Figure 8.14 – The scene with Off Mesh Links – NavMesh04-OffMeshLinks.scene

In this section, we will learn how to connect these two planes using **Off Mesh Links**.

Generated Off Mesh Links

Firstly, we use autogenerated Off Mesh Links to connect the two planes. To do that, we need to follow these steps:

1. Mark these two planes as **Off Mesh Link Generation** and **Static** in the property Inspector, as shown in the following screenshot:

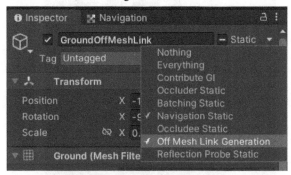

Figure 8.15 – Off Mesh Link Generation and Static

2. Go to the **Navigation** window and look at the properties on the **Bake** tab. You can set the distance threshold to autogenerate Off Mesh Links:

Figure 8.16 – Generated Off Mesh Links properties

3. Click on **Bake**, and you should have Off Mesh Links connecting the two planes, like this:

Figure 8.17 – Generated Off Mesh Links

4. Now, our AI agents can find the path between the planes. But first, ensure that the tanks have **Jump** enabled in the **Area Mask** property of the **Nav Mesh Agent** component, as shown in *Figure 8.18*:

Figure 8.18 – The Area Mask configuration for the Tanks

If everything is correct, agents will essentially jump to the other plane once they reach the edge of the plane and find an **Off Mesh Link** component. But, of course, if jumping agents are not what we want (after all, who has ever seen a jumping tank?), we should instead put a bridge for the Agents to cross.

Manual Off Mesh Links

If we don't want to generate Off Mesh Links along the edge and, instead, we want the Agents to reach a certain point before teleporting to the other side, then we need to set up the Off Mesh Links manually, as we can see in *Figure 8.19*:

Figure 8.19 – Manual Off Mesh Links setup

Execute the following steps to set up the Off Mesh Links manually:

1. We initialize a scene with a significant gap between the two planes. Then, we place two pairs of sphere entities on each side of the plane.

2. Choose a sphere and add an **Off Mesh Link** component by navigating to **Component | Navigation | Off Mesh Link**. We only need to add this component to one sphere.

3. Next, drag and drop the first sphere to the **Start** property and the other sphere to the **End** property:

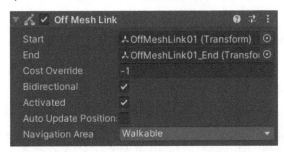

Figure 8.20 – Off Mesh Link component

4.   Go to the **Navigation** window and bake the scene.

Figure 8.21 – Manually generated Off Mesh Links

5.   The manual **Off Mesh Links** now connect the two planes, and AI agents can use them to traverse terrain, even in the presence of gaps.

> **Info**
>
> You can find Unity's official reference for Off Mesh Links at `https://docs.unity3d.com/Manual/nav-CreateOffMeshLink.html`.

This last demo concludes our exploration of Unity's NavMeshes. You should now know all the basics of this vital tool for AI character development.

Summary

In this chapter, we learned how to generate and use NavMeshes to implement pathfinding for our games. First, we studied how to set up different navigation layers with varying costs for pathfinding. Then, using the destination property, we used the **Nav Mesh Agent** component to find the path and move toward the target. Next, we set up Off Mesh Links to connect the gaps between the NavMeshes using the autogeneration feature and a manual setup with the **Off Mesh Link** component.

With all this information, we can now easily create simple games with a reasonably complicated AI. For example, you can try to set the destination property of AI tanks to the player's tank's position and make them follow it. Then, using simple FSMs, they can start attacking the player once they reach a certain distance. FSMs have taken us far, but they have their limits. In the next chapter, we will learn about Behavior Trees and how we can use them to make AI decisions in even the most complex games.

Part 3:
Advanced AI

In this part, we will learn more complex techniques for creating characters' behavior and decision-making abilities, including behavior trees and machine learning-powered agents.

We will cover the following chapters in this part:

9

Behavior Trees

In a preceding chapter, we saw a basic but effective way to implement and manage character states and behaviors: **finite state machines** (**FSMs**). FSMs are simple to implement and intuitive, but they have a fatal flaw: it is tough to make them scale once there are many states and transitions. For example, imagine a character that behaves differently depending on its health and mana (high, medium, or low). We have a state in which both health and mana are high, one in which health is medium and mana is high, one in which they are both medium, and so on. In total, we have nine states just for those. If we add other conditions (such as player proximity, time of day, equipment, player's score, or whatever you may imagine), the number of states grows exponentially.

Luckily, we have a solution: **behavior trees** (**BTs**). In essence, BTs are just another way to visualize complex FSMs, but they are fast, provide reusability, and are easy to maintain. After their introduction in 2004 with *Halo 2*, they quickly became the preferred decision-making technique in games.

In this chapter, we will be doing the following:

- Exploring the basic principles of BTs, knowledge that you will be able to transfer to any BT plugin available for Unity (or other game engines)

- Implementing a small demo based on a popular free Unity plugin for BTs: **Behavior Bricks**

Technical requirements

For this chapter, you need Unity3D 2022 and the free plugin for Unity, *Behavior Bricks*. Don't worry, we will see how to install this plugin together. You can find the example project described in this chapter in the `Chapter 9` folder in the book repository here: `https://github.com/PacktPublishing/Unity-Artificial-Intelligence-Programming-Fifth-Edition/tree/main/Chapter09`.

Introduction to BTs

A BT is a hierarchical tree of nodes that controls the AI character's behavior flow. It can also be used to coordinate groups of characters (for example, to model the attack pattern of a small platoon), or even disembodied agents such as an AI story director.

When we execute a BT's node, the node can return three states: **success**, **failure**, or **running** (if the node's execution is spread over multiple frames, for instance, if it plays an animation). When the BT executor runs a tree, it starts from the root and executes every node in order, according to rules written in the nodes themselves.

A node can be of three types:

- A **task** (a node without children), also called a **leaf**.
- A **decorator** (a node with a single child)
- A **composite** (a node with multiple children)

In general, leaves represent the *Action* that the characters can do or know (that is why they are commonly called an **Action** or **Task**); they may be actions such as **GoToTarget**, **OpenDoor**, **Jump**, or **TakeCover**, but also things like **IsObjectNear?** or **IsHealthLow?**. These actions depend on the character, the game, and the general game implementation.

A **decorator** is a node that modifies (decorates) the sub-tree under it (therefore, it can decorate both composite and task nodes). For example, a standard decorator is the **Negate** node. The node inverts the return value of the sub-tree; for instance, if the sub-tree returns *Success*, the decorator returns *Failure* and vice versa (of course, if the sub-tree returns *Running*, the decorator returns *Running* as well). Another everyday decorator is **Repeat**, a node that repeats its sub-tree a certain number of times.

Instead, a **composite** node represents a node with multiple children, and it is the most interesting case. There are two common composite nodes: **Sequence**, which runs all its children in order and returns *Success* if—and only if—all its children return *Success*, and **Selector**, which tries to execute all its children in order but returns *Success* as soon as one of its children returns *Success*. However, many BT implementations contain many more composite nodes (such as nodes that run their children in parallel or according to some dynamic priority value; we will see an example of such a node in the demo).

Of course, this tree structure is not enough. Nodes need to exchange information with each other or with the game world. For instance, a **GoToTarget** node needs to know the target and its location; an **IsObjectClose?** node needs to know which object we are referring to and what distance we consider close. Naturally, we could write a **GoToX** node for each object in the game (such as **GoToTree01** and **GoToDoor23**), but you can easily imagine that this becomes messy very quickly.

For this reason, all the BT implementations contain a data structure called **Blackboard**. As in a real-life physical blackboard, every node can write and read data into it; we just need to specify where to look for each node.

A simple example – a patrolling robot

Let's look at this example (which we will later implement in Unity). Imagine a patrolling robot that shoots anything that gets near it but works only during the daytime. We show the possible BT for this kind of agent in the following diagram:

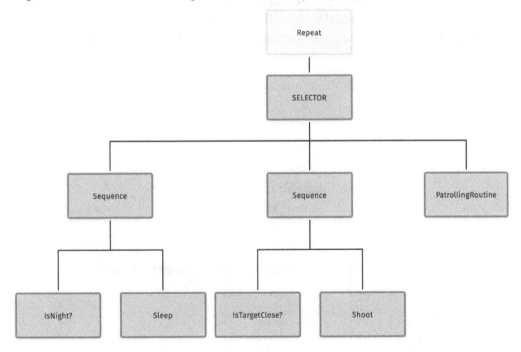

Figure 9.1 – Example BT for a simplified day-only patrolling robot

Let's run this BT, assuming that the target is close and it is not night:

1. The first node is a **Repeat** decorator; it does nothing but cycle the BTs, therefore, we can ignore it for now.

2. The **SELECTOR** node starts executing its first child; we go down to the left.

3. We are now at the first **Sequence** node; again, we execute the first node. **IsNight?** returns *Failure* (because it is not night!). Whenever one node returns *Failure*, the whole **Sequence** node returns *Failure*.

4. We traverse back up the tree to the **SELECTOR** node; now, we go to the second branch.

5. Again, we execute **Sequence**.

6. This time, however, **IsTargetClose?** returns *Success*, so we can proceed to the next node, **Shoot**, which runs a game function spawning an in-game projectile.

The pattern of **Sequence | Condition | Action** is equivalent to if *Condition* is *Success* then *Action*. This pattern is so common that many BT implementations allow you to stack the *Condition* and the *Action* together. Therefore, we can rewrite the tree as follows:

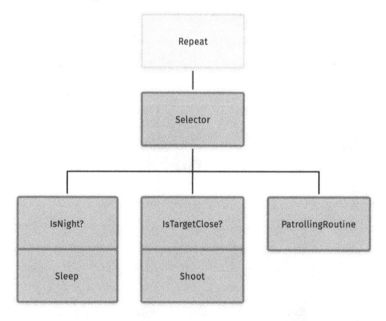

Figure 9.2 – A simplified BT

This tree is the same as the previous one but with a simplified Sequence pattern.

Implementing a BT in Unity with Behavior Bricks

Behavior Bricks is a robust but free BT implementation for Unity developed by the Complutense University of Madrid in Spain. Using Behavior Bricks, you can start using BTs in your projects without implementing BTs from scratch. It also has a visual editor where you can drop and connect nodes without any additional code.

Follow these steps to install Behavior Bricks:

1. We need to go to the *Unity Asset Store* by going on the website `https://assetstore.unity.com/`.

2. Search for `Behavior Bricks`.

3. Click on **Add to My Assets**. Once it's done, we can import it into our project.

Figure 9.3 – Behavior Bricks Asset Store main page

4. Go to **Package Manager** (**Window | Package Manager**).

5. Go to **My Assets**.

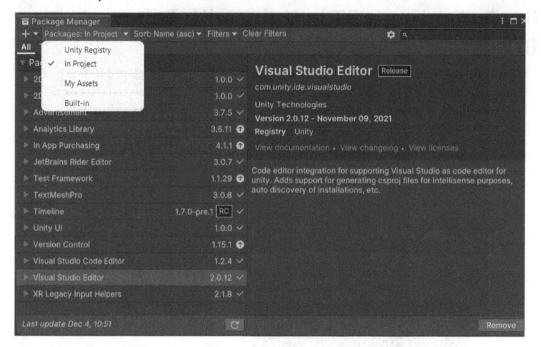

Figure 9.4 – The Package Manager window

6. Import the **Behavior Bricks** package by clicking on the **Import** button.

Figure 9.5 – Behavior Bricks in Package Manager

At this point, Behavior Bricks is ready to go, and we can proceed with our demo. The following steps give you a brief idea of the steps to follow:

1. Set up the scene.

2. Implement a day/night cycle.

3. Design the enemy behavior.

4. Implement the nodes.

5. Build the tree.

6. Attach the BT to the enemy.

Now, let's take a look at each of these steps individually.

Set up the scene

Let's follow a step-by-step process to do this:

1. We start by adding the game objects to the scene. We add a big plane to the scene, we add a `Box Collider` that encloses the entire plane, and we call it `Floor` (you may also add a texture if you like; be creative as it helps to have fun with these simple demos).

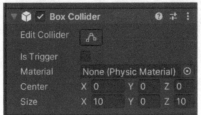

Figure 9.6 – Example of the Floor Box Collider

2. We add a sphere and a cube; we call the sphere *Player* and the cube *Enemy*. In the *Enemy*, we add another empty object and move it just outside the cube. We call it `shootPoint`, and it represents the placeholder for where the enemy shoots.

3. Then, place all these objects on the floor; you should have something similar to the following:

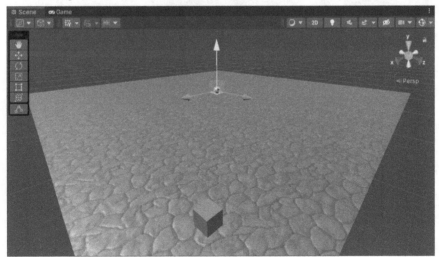

Figure 9.7 – The scene of our demo

4. Now, because we want the player and the enemy to move around, we need to create a NavMesh as described in *Chapter 8*, *Navigation Mesh*. Remember to add the **NavMesh Agent** component to both *Player* and *Enemy*!

5. Finally, if it is not present, add the **MainLight** tag to the *Direct Light* object.

Implement a day/night cycle

In this demo, we want to implement a basic day/night cycle. To do that, we attach the script `DayNightCycle.cs` to the *Direct Light* object. As with many scripts in this demo, we adapt the code from the *Quick Start Guide* provided by Behavior Bricks:

```
using UnityEngine;

public class DayNightCycle : MonoBehaviour {
    public event System.EventHandler OnChanged;
    public float dayDuration = 10.0f;
    public bool IsNight { get; private set; }
    public Color nightColor = Color.white * 0.1f;
    private Color dayColor;
    private Light lightComponent;

    void Start() {
        lightComponent = GetComponent<Light>();
        dayColor = lightComponent.color;
    }

    void Update() {
        float lightIntensity = 0.5f + Mathf.Sin(Time.time *
          2.0f * Mathf.PI / dayDuration) / 2.0f;

        bool shouldBeNight = lightIntensity < 0.3f;
        if (IsNight != shouldBeNight) {
            IsNight = shouldBeNight;
            // Invoke event handler (if set).
            OnChanged?.Invoke(this,
                System.EventArgs.Empty);
        }

        lightComponent.color = Color.Lerp(nightColor,
```

```
            dayColor, lightIntensity);        }
  }
```

This script implements a typical day/night cycle. The way it works is quite intuitive. Let's have a look:

- At each `Update` step, we update the `lightIntensity` variable according to a sinusoidal wave.

- The variable cycles from 0 to 1 and, when the value is smaller than 0.3, we decide that it is nighttime.

- Finally, we update the light color according to the `lightIntensity` value, interpolating the day and night colors.

- Note the `onChanged` event. We call it every time we switch from daytime to nighttime, and from nighttime to daytime. Later, we use this event to create an **IsNight** node in the BT.

Design the enemy behavior

Now, it is time to design the enemy behavior. We need to do this before writing a single line of code. For this demo, we will adapt the code and assets provided by the example project in the Behavior Bricks *Quick Start Guide*. For more information, you can refer to it at this URL: `http://bb.padaonegames.com/doku.php?id=quick:program`.

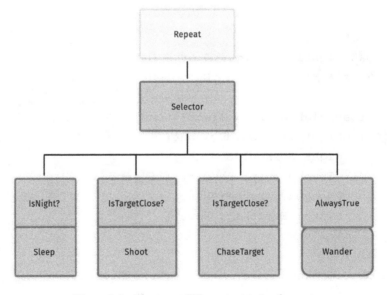

Figure 9.8 – The target BT we want to implement

The BT in *Figure 9.8* describes the following behavior:

- If it is night, the enemy is deactivated.

- If the target is very close, the enemy shoots at the target.

- If the target is further away, the enemy chases the target.

- Otherwise, the enemy just wanders around.

There are two important things to note:

- First, the two **IsTargetClose?** nodes differ in the value we consider close. In particular, we want to shoot the target only if we are close to it; otherwise, we just start chasing it.

- Second, and most importantly, the order of the nodes matters. Because the **Selector** works from left to right and stops at the first *Success*, we cannot put **ChaseTarget** before **Shoot**. Otherwise, the enemy will never shoot!

As a rule of thumb, we need to order conditions from the highest to the lowest priority. In fact, in the example, we put at the very end the action to execute when everything else fails (**AlwaysTrue** is a condition that always succeeds and works like the *else* branch of an *if* condition).

Note that **Wander** is in a different color because it is not a node but another BT. The lovely property of BTs is that you can reuse common BTs as nodes inside more complex BTs. The Wander BT simply makes the enemy move randomly on the map; fortunately, Behavior Bricks already includes it, so we don't need to implement it!

Implementing the nodes

After we have made a plan for our BT, the next step is to check whether our BT implementation of choice (in our case, Behavior Bricks) already includes some of the nodes we need. Of course, we want to reuse as many pre-made nodes as possible. Reading the Behavior Bricks documentation, we can see that it already includes nodes such as **IsTargetClose**, **MoveToGameObject**, **Wander**, and **AlwaysTrue**, plus, of course, **Repeat** and **Selector**.

Therefore, we need to write all the other tasks. Note that Behavior Bricks tasks are not MonoBehaviors; therefore, we do not need to attach them to some object in the scene. We only need to put the scripts in any folder in our project's assets, and we are good. Let's look at a step-by-step process to do this:

1. Let's start with the **ShootOnce** action by creating a `ShootOnce.cs` file in the project assets. First, we create a simple `Action` attribute called `ShootOnce` that, as the name says, shoots a single bullet:

```
using UnityEngine;

using Padal.BBCore;
using Padal.BBCore.Tasks;
using BBUnity.Actions;

[Action("Chapter09/ShootOnce")]
[Help("Clone a 'bullet' and shoots it through the Forward
axis with the specified velocity.")]
public class ShootOnce : GOAction {
    // ….
}
```

In the beginning, we import Behavior Bricks modules. Then, we create the `ShootOnce` class by extending the generic `GOAction` class.

Note the class attributes; Behavior Bricks uses them to populate the BT visual editor. In the `Action` attribute, we specify that `Action` is an action, and we put it in the `Chapter09` collection with the name `ShootOnce`. The `Help` attribute is just a documentation string describing the action's purpose.

2. We describe the class attributes as usual. The only difference is that we decorate each attribute with the `InParam` attribute, which specifies that the BT executor needs to retrieve the following value from the blackboard:

```
[InParam("shootPoint")]
public Transform shootPoint;

[InParam("bullet")]
public GameObject bullet;
```

```
[InParam("velocity", DefaultValue = 30f)]
public float velocity;
```

For this action, we need a `Bullet` prefab, a place to instantiate the bullet (`shootPoint`) and the bullet velocity. Later, we will see how to set them up from the visual interface.

3. Now, it is time to write the real meat:

```
public override void OnStart() {
    if (shootPoint == null) {
        shootPoint =
            gameObject.transform.Find("shootPoint");
        if (shootPoint == null) {
            Debug.LogWarning("Shoot point not
                specified. ShootOnce will not work for "
                + gameObject.name);
        }
    }
    base.OnStart();
}


public override TaskStatus OnUpdate() {
    if (shootPoint == null || bullet == null) {
        return TaskStatus.FAILED;
    }
    GameObject newBullet = Object.Instantiate(
        bullet, shootPoint.position,
        shootPoint.rotation *
        bullet.transform.rotation );
    if (newBullet.GetComponent<Rigidbody>() == null) {
        newBullet.AddComponent<Rigidbody>();
    }
    newBullet.GetComponent<Rigidbody>().velocity =
        velocity * shootPoint.forward;
    return TaskStatus.COMPLETED;
}
```

Every Behavior Bricks node contains some default method called during the BT execution. We can overwrite them in our custom implementations. In this example, we see two of them: `OnStart` and `OnUpdate`. They are used very similarly to how we use `Start` and `Update` in `MonoBehavior`:

- The BT executor calls `OnStart` when the game creates the BT. In it, we initialize all the references we need. In this case, we get a reference to the `shootPoint` object. Note also that we must call `base.Onstart()` to initialize the base class.

- In `OnUpdate`, we write the intended action for the node, that is, what we want this node to do when the BT executor invokes it. In this case, the code is self-explanatory: we create a bullet and shoot it at the velocity stored in the settings.

If there is no problem, we mark the node as complete (so that the BT knows that it is a *Success*); otherwise (for example, if there is no `shootPoint` value), we mark the node as *Failed*.

4. Now that we have a base class for shooting once, we can create a new `Action` attribute for shooting continuously. Let's create a `Shoot.cs` file with the following content:

```
Using UnityEngine;


using Pada1.BBCore
using Pada1.BBCore.Tasks;


[Action("Chapter09/Shoot")]
[Help("Periodically clones a 'bullet' and shoots it
through the Forward axis with the specified velocity.
This action never ends.")]
public class Shoot : ShootOnce {
    [InParam("delay", DefaultValue = 1.0f)]
    public float delay;

    // Time since the last shoot.
    private float elapsedTime = 0;

    public override TaskStatus OnUpdate() {
        if (delay > 0) {
            elapsedTime += Time.deltaTime;
```

```
        if (elapsedTime >= delay) {
            elapsedTime = 0;
            return TaskStatus.RUNNING;
        }


    }

        base.OnUpdate();
        return TaskStatus.RUNNING;      }
    }
```

This class simply extends the ShootOnce class, adds a delay attribute (the time between consecutive shots), and then continuously reruns its parent class (ShootOnce). Note that this Action always returns RUNNING, meaning that it never completes as long as the BT selects it.

5. In the same way, we can create the remaining Action attribute. For instance, the SleepForever action is very straightforward: it just does nothing and suspends the execution of the BTs. Note that the class extends BasePrimitiveAction, which is the most basic form of Action in Behavior Bricks:

```
using Padal.BBCore;
using Padal.BBCore.Framework;
using Padal.BBCore.Tasks;


[Action("Chapter09/SleepForever")]
[Help("Low-cost infinite action that never ends. It does
not consume CPU at all.")]


public class SleepForever : BasePrimitiveAction {
    public override TaskStatus OnUpdate() {
        return TaskStatus.SUSPENDED;
    }
}
```

6. Finally, we need to implement IsNightCondition. We show the IsNightCondition code in the following listing:

```
using Padal.BBCore;
using Padal.BBCore.Framework;
```

```csharp
using Pada1.BBCore.Tasks;
using UnityEngine;

[Condition("Chapter09/IsNight")]
[Help("Checks whether it is night time.")]
public class IsNightCondition : ConditionBase {
    private DayNightCycle light;

    public override bool Check() {
        return SearchLight() && light.IsNight;
    }

    public override TaskStatus
      MonitorCompleteWhenTrue() {
        if (Check()) {
            return TaskStatus.COMPLETED;
        }
        if (light != null) {
            light.OnChanged += OnSunset;
        }
        return TaskStatus.SUSPENDED;
    }

    public override TaskStatus MonitorFailWhenFalse()
    {
        if (!Check()) {
            return TaskStatus.FAILED;
        }
        light.OnChanged += OnSunrise;
        return TaskStatus.SUSPENDED;
    }

    /// ...

    private bool searchLight() {
        if (light != null) {
```

```
        return true;
    }
    GameObject lightGO =
        GameObject.FindGameObjectWithTag(
        "MainLight");
    if (lightGO == null) {
        return false;
    }
    light = lightGO.GetComponent<DayNightCycle>();
    return light != null;
    }
}
```

This class is more complex than the others, so let's go slow. First of all, IsNightCondition extends ConditionBase, which is a basic condition template in Behavior Bricks. This class does a simple job: on start, it searches for a light with the MainLight tag. If that exists, it takes its DayNightCycle reference, stores it in the light variable, and registers with the OnChanged event. Then, every time we ask for this condition, we check whether the isNight variable in light is true or false (see the Check method).

However, checking this every time would be very inefficient, in general. So, the BaseCondition class contains two helpful functions:

- MonitorCompleteWhenTrue is a function that is called by the BT executor when the last returned value is false and, in practice, sets up a system that suspends BT execution until the variable becomes true again.

- MonitorFailWhenFalse is a dual function: it is called when the monitored value is true and suspends BT execution until the variable switches to false.

For instance, let's look at MonitorCompleteWhenTrue. If Check is true (so it is night), we simply return Complete; otherwise, we register the OnSunset function with the OnChanged event. When the day/night cycle switches from day to night, OnSunset is called and, in turn, EndMonitorWithSuccess is called. MonitorFailWhenFalse works in the same way but in the opposite direction (monitoring when we pass from night to day):

```
public void OnSunset(object sender,
                     System.EventArgs night) {
    light.OnChanged -= OnSunset;
```

```
        EndMonitorWithSuccess();
    }


    public void OnSunrise(object sender,
                        System.EventArgs e) {
        light.OnChanged -= OnSunrise;
        EndMonitorWithFailure();
    }
```

In the preceding code block, there are the two OnSunset and OnSunrise event handlers included in the class. As usual, you can find the complete commented code in the book's repository.

Building the tree

Now that we have our nodes, we need to assemble the tree. To do that, follow these steps:

1. Right-click in the **Inspector** and go to the **Create** sub-menu.

2. Then, select **Behavior Tree**.

3. Choose a location and save.

4. An empty editor window should show onscreen; this is the tree editor.

5. You can right-click anywhere and start adding and connecting nodes.

6. To implement our tree, you need to recreate the tree shown in the following screenshot:

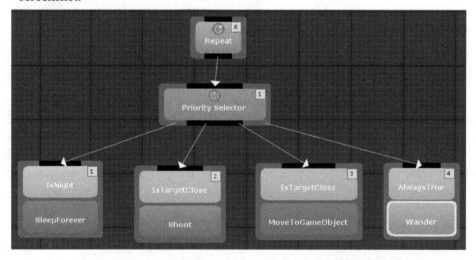

Figure 9.9 – The enemy BT in the Behavior Bricks editor

7. Select all the nodes, one at a time, and look for the input parameters; these are the parameters we specified in our classes. These parameters may be **CONSTANT**, meaning that we directly write a value for them, or a **BLACKBOARD** reference.

8. We need to set up the parameters with the following values:

    - In the first `IsTargetClose`, we specify the blackboard player as `target` and the constant 7 as `closeDistance` (if the player is not listed, click on **New Parameter**).

    - In the second `IsTargetClose`, we specify the blackboard player as `target` and the constant 20 as `closeDistance`.

    - In `Shoot`, we need to set 30 as the delay, the blackboard `shootPoint` as `shootPoint` (you probably need to create it with **New Parameter**), the blackboard bullet as the `bullet` prefab, and the constant 30 as velocity.

    - In `MoveToGameObject`, the target is the player value in the blackboard.

9. In `Wander`, we set a new blackboard parameter (`floor`) as `wanderArea`.

Attach the BT to the enemy

Now, it is time to attach this BT to the enemy's BT executor. For that, follow these steps:

1. Select the **Enemy** game object and add the **Behavior Executor** component to it.

2. In the **Behavior** field, drag and drop the BT we created before.

3. In **Behavior Parameters**, a list of all the blackboard parameters we defined in the previous step (`player`, `floor`, the enemy `shootPoint` firing location, and `bullet`) should appear.

4. Fill them with the appropriate objects, as shown in *Figure 9.10*:

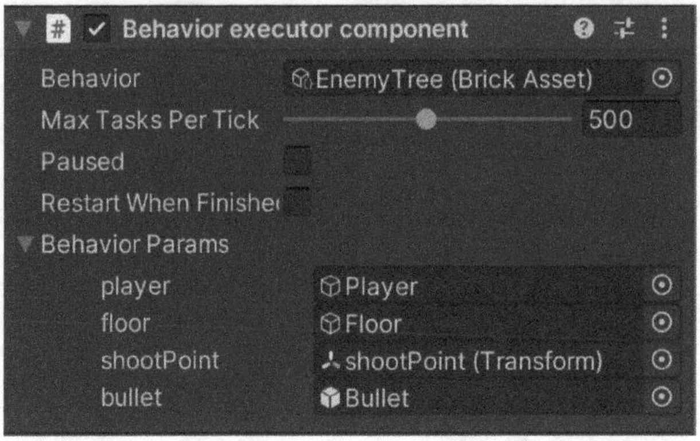

Figure 9.10 – The behavior executor component

At this point, the enemy should be ready to go. Click **Play** and you should see the enemy wandering around and, when close enough to the player, start chasing and shooting at it. Note that we did not implement a controller for the player, therefore, to change its position you need to edit the player in the Scene view (or attach one of the control scripts we developed in the previous chapters). For more details, look at the code included in this book.

Now that we have completed our first BT, what if we want to replicate with Behavior Bricks the same AI that we developed in *Chapter 2, Finite State Machines*, using an FSM? Try that as an exercise.

Summary

In this chapter, we explored the general background behind any BT implementation. We saw what a BT is, what its basic components are, and how can we use a BT to describe game character behavior. Then, we implemented a demo using a free plugin called Behavior Bricks. In the demo, we created the behavior for a simple scenario: the player and a patrolling robot. We also implemented a day/night cycle to spice up the scenario.

BTs are the cornerstones of modern AI for game characters. Implementation details and deeper examples would require a full book to explain them fully. Luckily, the web is full of resources for the curious reader.

Now, we will take a break from AI character design by looking at a different application of AI in games. In the next chapter, we will look at the fascinating field of procedural content generation.

Further reading

- The official Behavior Bricks project page from the Complutense University of Madrid in Spain: `http://gaia.fdi.ucm.es/research/bb/`.

- Behavior Bricks official documentation: `http://bb.padaonegames.com/doku.php`.

- Chris Simpson (the developer of *Project Zomboid*) wrote a nice explanation of BTs on Gamasutra: `https://www.gamasutra.com/blogs/ChrisSimpson/20140717/221339/Behavior_trees_for_AI_How_they_work.php`.

- *Chapter 6* of *GameAI Pro*, which explores many implementation details of BTs (in C++), is free and available at the following link: `https://www.gameaipro.com/ GameAIPro/GameAIPro_Chapter06_The_Behavior_Tree_Starter_Kit.pdf`.

10
Procedural Content Generation

Game AI is not only used to tell NPCs where to go or what to do. We can also use game AI to create parts of our games, to generate assets or music, to adapt the game story to the player's actions as a movie director, and even to generate narrative arcs and character backstories entirely. In the general AI world, this is the topic of **Computational Creativity**, a branch of AI concerned with the design of algorithms to enhance human creativity or completely automate tasks requiring human-level creativity.

The scope of computational creativity is broad and cutting edge. It started in 1952 with Alan Turing writing the first algorithm capable of generating love letters. Today, it continues with powerful machine-learning-powered algorithms attempting to write poetry, compose symphonies, or produce astounding visual art pieces.

Luckily for us, in games, we are interested in a more limited subset of this discipline. We are not interested in producing algorithms with human-level creativity (with all the philosophical questions attached to this endeavor). Instead, we only want to write algorithms that can automatically expand the contents of our game, be it by generating thousands of random dungeons, hundreds of new weapons, models of alien flora and animals, or anything else. This is called **Procedural Content Generation** (**PCG**), and it is a prominent protagonist of videogame automation.

In this chapter, we will cover the following topics:

- Understanding the basic concept of PCG in video games

- Dipping our toes into PCG by implementing a random generator for the names of Goblin NPCs

- Implementing a simple cave/dungeon generator

Technical requirements

 For this chapter, you just need Unity3D 2022. You can find the example project described in this chapter in the `Chapter 10` folder in the book's repository: `https://github. com/PacktPublishing/Unity-Artificial-Intelligence-Programming- Fifth-Edition/tree/main/Chapter10`.

Understanding Procedural Content Generation in games

As discussed in the introduction, we are refering to all the algorithms that can generate game content at runtime with PCG algorithms. A PCG algorithm may create the level design, weapons, graphical assets, musical themes, enemies, NPCs, characters' backstories, and whatever else you set your mind on. If you think about any element in a game, there is a chance that there is at least one game that attempted to generate it procedurally. But why should you?

Nowadays, PCG has become a synonym of *random* for the general public. Many games advertise having *procedurally generated levels* as a way of saying that they offer thousands of different levels that change at every playthrough. While PCG *may* indicate some process of causality, it is worth noting that that's just part of the PCG landscape (even if, probably, the most marketable). More properly, PCG is the opposite of randomness: it is an algorithm that very deterministically starts from a *seed* and produces some content (but, of course, if we use a random seed, we obtain random outputs).

There are two principal use cases for PCG:

- The first is to use PCG to generate *persistent content that is impossible to pre-generate during development*. If the content is too big to be stored in a file or manual generation requires too much effort, we may have this necessity. For instance, the original space simulation game *Elite* (1985) used PCG to store 8 galaxies with a 256-star system each (in addition to the game code) in just 32 KB. With the increase in available disk space, this use case is no longer the biggest. However, it is still possible to find uses. The new version of Elite, called *Elite: Dangerous*, released in 2014, used the same approach to represent a real-scale copy of the Milky Way with the astounding number of 400 billion fully explorable star systems. Note that there is no randomness involved: the galaxy is persistent, and all the players share it in the game. It would be simply impossible to store the individual data for each star system on disk.

> **More Info**
>
> You can find an inspiring and exciting analysis of the generative algorithm of the original Elite game at this URL: `https://www.gamedeveloper.com/design/algorithms-for-an-infinite-universe`.

- The second is the most common use case: *add variety and replayability to a game by casually generating content at every playthrough*. Rogue-like games popularized this PCG use, but the most successful videogame using PCG to forge a different random world at every new run is, without doubt, Minecraft. With PCG, you do not need to craft every level manually or to design hundreds of different levels: you just need to specify the *rules* and let the software automatically generate a wide variety of levels or weapons.

Now that we understand *why*, let's explore some different types of PCG algorithms.

Kinds of Procedural Content Generation

During the long history of game development, PCG has been used for a wide variety of tasks. As a result, we can identify six applications of PCG:

- **Runtime Content Generation**: This is the type of PCG we instinctively think about when we hear PCG. It includes the generation at runtime of the game contents. The creation of random worlds in *Minecraft* or random maps and weapons in *Diablo* are typical examples of this category.

- **Offline Content Generation**: This is the type of PCG we use during development. Even if we do not plan to give the players the ability to explore a randomly generated world, PCG is still useful for designers and developers. For instance, if we create a forest, we can use PCG to create 3D models of trees with different shapes (**SpeedTree** is a standard tool used for this purpose). We can also use PCG to kickstart the manual design of levels. Suppose we want to design an island. We may start by generating a simple random PCG island, then choose the one that most inspires us, and finally apply manual editing and modeling to it to create the final island we will ship in the final game. There are many other applications of PCG for design tools, but they go way out of the scope of this chapter.

- **Player-Mediated Content Generation**: These types of PCG algorithms use the players' input as a source of *randomness*.

- **Dynamic Systems**: This kind of PCG generates NPCs' behavior and a narrative background by simulating dynamic systems. A notable example is the A-Life system of the game called *S.T.A.L.K.E.R.*. In the game, the A-Life system simulates the life cycle of thousands of inhabitants of the game world. Consequently, the system provides infinite non-scripted characters to interact with and unlimited side-quests.

But that is enough theory for now. Let's start coding.

Implementing a simple goblin name generator

In the previous section, we explained that the primary purpose of PCG is to provide variety while removing from the developer the burden of scripting such variety by hand. So, imagine that we are developing an old-school RPG, and we want the players to be able to interact with the NPC characters of a goblin encampment.

In the encampment, there are hundreds of goblins, and we really want to avoid coming up with the name and the occupation of every one of them. Not only because it's boring and time-consuming, but if we're going to have random encounters with goblins in the game world, we need to have the ability to create new goblins on the fly.

Fortunately, we have a more fun (for us) solution: to write an algorithm generating a huge number of random goblin characters.

Generating goblin names

In order to generate something, we need to find some kind of *generative rule*. To find such a rule, the best thing is to look at different examples of what we want to generate and try to figure out if some pattern connects them. For example, for goblin names, we can look for insight in a bunch of goblin names from World of Warcraft.

Let's look at some of them: *Grizzle Gearslip*, *Hobart Grapplehammer*, and *Helix Blackfuse*. Continuing with this list, we may identify a common pattern:

- The names are composed of two or three syllables.

- The syllables have similar sounds, such as *Bax*, *Griz*, *Hel*, *Hob*, and so on.

- The surname is always composed of the name of an object or an adjective (gear, grapple, black, bolt) followed by a verb.

- The theme of the surnames is usually related to mechanical engineering.

That's enough to get started. We create a new scene, and we create a new script called GoblinNameGenerator, and we paste inside the following code:

```
class GoblinNameGenerator {
    static string[] NameDatabase1 = { "Ba", "Bax", "Dan",
        "Fi", "Fix", "Fiz", }; //... and more

    static string[] NameDatabase2 = { "b", "ba", "be",
        "bi", "d", "da", "de","di", }; // ... and more

    static string[] NameDatabase3 = { "ald", "ard", "art",
        "az", "azy", "bit","bles", "eek", "eka", "et",
        "ex", "ez", "gaz", "geez", "get", "giez",
        "iek", }; // ... and more

    static string[] SurnameDatabase1 = { "Bolt", "Boom",
        "Bot", "Cog", "Copper","Damp", "Dead", "Far", "Fast",
        "Fiz", "Fizz", "Fizzle", "Fuse", "Gear",
        "Giga", "Gold", "Grapple" }; // ... and more

    static string[] SurnameDatabase2 = { "basher", "blade",
        "blast", "blaster","bolt", "bomb", "boot", "bottom",
        "bub", "button", "buttons", "cash",
        "clamp", }; // ... and more

    private static string RandomInArray(string[] array) {
        return array[Random.Range(0, array.Length)];
```

```
    }

    public static string RandomGoblinName() {
        return RandomInArray(NameDatabase1) +
          RandomInArray(NameDatabase2) +
            RandomInArray(NameDatabase3) + " " +
            RandomInArray(SurnameDatabase1) +
            RandomInArray(SurnameDatabase2);
    }
}
```

This code straightforwardly converts the rules of goblin names into a procedural algorithm. The `NameDatabase1`, `NameDatabase2`, and `NameDatabase3` arrays contain the first, middle, and last syllables of the first name. Similarly, `SurnameDatabase1` and `SurnameDatabase2` have the two parts of a goblin's surname. To generate the name, we chose a random piece from each list, and we put everything together.

Completing the goblin description

Now that we have a name, we need only other small details. So, let's create an empty object and attach to it a new `MonoBehavior` instance named `GoblinWriter`.

This new script contains the following code:

```
using System.Collections;
using System.Collections.Generic;
using UnityEngine;

public class GoblinWriter : MonoBehaviour {

    public TMPro.TextMeshProUGUI textMesh;
    public List<string> goblinJobs;
    public int goblinMaxAge = 200;

    void Start() {
        UpdateString();
    }
```

```
    void Update() {
        if (Input.GetKeyDown(KeyCode.Space)) {
            UpdateString();
        }
    }


    void UpdateString() {
        string goblinName =
          GoblinNameGenerator.RandomGoblinName();
        string goblinAge = Random.Range(20,
          goblinMaxAge).ToString();
        string goblinJob = goblinJobs[Random.Range(0,
          goblinJobs.Count)];
        textMesh.text = $"{goblinName} is a {goblinAge}
          years old goblin {goblinJob}.";
    }
}
```

The script has three exposed properties. The first, textMesh, is a reference to the TextMesh element that will show the text on screen (you can create one by going to **GameObject | UI | Text – TextMeshPro**). The second, goblinJobs, stores a list of jobs we want to give to the goblins. As you can see in *Figure 10.1*, I added four jobs: **warrior**, **archer**, **blacksmith**, and **shaman**. The third, goblinMaxAge, represents the maximum age for my goblins.

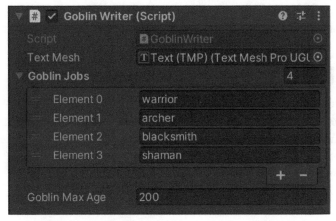

Figure 10.1 – The Goblin Writer script in the Inspector

Whenever we call UpdateString (that is, at the start of the game and every time we press *Spacebar*), we simply extract a value from the set of possible values for the age, the job, and the name, and construct a string. Once we have everything set up, we can run the demo, and we should see a new goblin description every time we press *Spacebar* (*Figure 10.2*).

Figure 10.2 – One of the many random goblins we can generate

The example is simple, but it is an effective way to add variety to any game.

Info

The Dungeon Master manual of the fifth edition of Dungeon & Dragons contains several examples of this kind of *composition and randomness-driven* procedural generation. Inside it, you can find a lot of tables to generate treasures, weapons, side-quests, characters, and so on. Sure, it is designed to be used with pen and dice, but nothing stops you from translating paper algorithms into computer algorithms!

Now that we have a taste for procedural generation, let's step up the game. Let's introduce another handy tool for the PCG developer: Perlin noise.

Learning how to use Perlin noise

Perlin noise is an algorithm to define digital noise developed by Ken Perlin in 1983. It quickly became the de facto algorithm to generate natural-looking patterns in a considerable number of procedural content generation algorithms. For example, Perlin noise is used to create 3D landscapes, 2D textures, procedural animations, and much more.

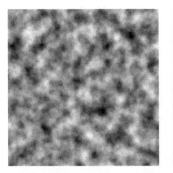

Figure 10.3 – The difference between Perlin noise (left) and white noise (right)

But what makes Perlin noise different from other noises? The short answer is that it looks more *natural*. This answer, however, just changes the question into *what does it mean to be more natural?* Let's imagine standard non-Perlin noise, for instance, a sequence of random numbers between 0 and 1. The sequence may be something like 0, 0.9, 0.2, 0.3, 0.95, and so on.

As you can see, the numbers can jump up and down without any criteria. If these numbers represent the position of a character in the game, the character will appear to teleport itself left and right frantically. That is not how things move in real life.

Perlin noise is different because, in the sequence of numbers, two consecutive numbers will always be close together. For example, after 0.9 we may have 0.91, 0.92, or 0.88 but never 0.1. The effect is like a buoy floating on the sea: it can move unpredictably left and right, up and down, but with a certain smoothness – a certain naturalness.

This looks perfect. However, how can we use Perlin noise in Unity? Luckily, Unity offers the Perlin noise algorithm as a built-in tool.

Built-in Unity Perlin noise

Unity offers a simple function to access Perlin noise:

```
Mathf.PerlinNoise(xCoord, yCoord);
```

Unity implements Perlin noise as an infinite 2D plane that you can randomly sample in code using the `Mathf.PerlinNoise` function. You can simply sample a random coordinate to get a *random* value on the Perlin noise plane.

> **Info**
>
> Note that Unity only offers you 2D Perlin noise. However, Perlin noise can be easily extended to 3D (for instance, to create volumetric smoke) or even four and more dimensions. If you need 3D Perlin noise, you need to develop the algorithm yourself or look for the many open source implementations you can find online (for instance, `https://gist.github.com/tntmeijs/6a3b4587ff7d38a6fa63e13f9d0ac46d`).

Imagine you want to create a random 2D texture using Unity's built-in Perlin noise. You can do that by starting at an arbitrary point (`xStart` and `yStart`) and then copying every surrounding point's value into the texture as you can see in the following example (the full `PerlinTexture.cs` file is included in the GitHub repository):

```
void CalculateNoise() {
    for (float y = 0.0f; y < noiseTex.height; y++) {
        for (float x = 0.0f; x < noiseTex.width; x++) {
            float xCoord =
                xOrg + x / noiseTex.width * scale;
            float yCoord =
                yOrg + y / noiseTex.height * scale;
            float value =
                Mathf.PerlinNoise(xCoord, yCoord);
            pix[(int)y * noiseTex.width + (int)x] =
                new Color(value, value, value);
        }
    }

    // Copy the pixel data to the texture and load it
    // into the GPU.
    noiseTex.SetPixels(pix);
    noiseTex.Apply();
}
```

However, we can also use 2D Perlin noise to generate 1D Perlin noise. In that case, we fix one coordinate (x or y) and we move the other in a straight line.

Suppose we want to animate a bobbing sphere, floating gently up and down like a balloon. We can do that by setting its *y* coordinate (canonically representing the up and down direction) to the value of the Perlin noise:

```
using UnityEngine;

public class Bobbling : MonoBehaviour {
    // Range over which height varies.
    public float heightScale = 1.0f;

    // Distance covered per second along X axis of Perlin
    // plane.
    public float xScale = 1.0f;

    void Update() {
        float height = heightScale *
          Mathf.PerlinNoise(Time.time * xScale, 0.0f);
        Vector3 pos = transform.position;
        pos.y = height;
        transform.position = pos;
    }
}
```

If you attach this small script to any object, you will see the object randomly moving up and down.

That's just the tip of the iceberg of Perlin noise application, but I hope that it will get you started. However, it is time for us to continue our journey into PCG. In the next section, we will generate a random cave using a new technique called **Cellular Automata**.

Generating random maps and caves

Another widespread application of PCG is the generation of maps and dungeons. For example, in the *roguelike* genre (a type of game that takes its name from the 1980s game *Rogue*), players face a randomly generated dungeon every time they start a game. Likewise, in *Minecraft*, players begin the game by generating a random world to explore and in which they need to survive. The examples are numerous – too many to be listed here.

There are significant numbers of algorithms to create game worlds. Some use fractal noise to generate random heightmaps. Some others create dungeon-like structures by creating random rooms and connecting them with corridors. Others build maps by randomly arranging manually premade rooms into a myriad of different combinations like in a puzzle (if you have ever played the tabletop game *Carcassonne*, you know what I am talking about).

This demo will explore a simple technique well suited for the generation of caves or natural-looking scenes, called **Cellular Automata**.

Cellular automata

Cellular Automata (CA) is not only a PCG algorithm. CA have been studied since 1950 as an abstract computational model. However, their popularity exploded only after the release of *Conway's Game of Life* in the 70s.

The basic idea of CA is to simulate the behavior of *cells* in a 2D grid. Each cell in the grid has two states: dead or alive. Each *cell* will die or live depending on rules that depend only on their neighbors.

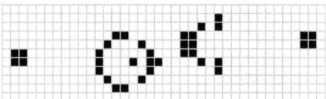

Figure 10.4 – A configuration of cells in the Game of Life

The behavior of a CA algorithm depends only on these evolution rules. So, we start from an initial configuration of alive and dead cells and then let the system evolve independently. In *Game of Life*, for example, we have four simple rules:

- Live cells with fewer than two live neighbors are underpopulated, and therefore they die.

- Live cells with two or three live neighbors keep living in the next generation.

- Live cells with more than three live neighbors are overpopulated, and therefore they die.

- Dead cells with exactly three live neighbors become alive again due to *reproduction*.

It turns out that these four simple rules are powerful enough to make the algorithm itself Turing complete. This means that it is possible to write a configuration of live and dead cells that, after applying the above four rules, is able to do any computation like a normal computer, for instance, multiplying numbers or playing chess. If you are interested in this, Paul Rendell has a detailed description of the pattern on his web page (http://rendell-attic.org/gol/tm.htm).

But let's come back to our goal. Luckily for us, we need to do something much more simple than implementing a CPU with our CA. In PCG, CA are an excellent choice because they are easy to implement and generate maps that look like natural environments such as deserts, caves, island archipelagos, and so on.

Implementing a cave generator

To implement our cave generator, we need two components:

- A component that generates and stores the map abstractly (for example, as an array of integers)

- A component that will render the abstract map in a visible 3D object in the game

So, let's start by implementing the first component. We'll call it CaveGenerator:

```
using UnityEngine;
using System;

public class CaveGenerator : MonoBehaviour {

    [SerializeField]
    private int width;

    [SerializeField]
    private int height;

    [SerializeField]
    private int seed;

    [SerializeField]
    private bool useRandomSeed;
```

```
    private int[,] map;


void Start() {
    InitializeRandomGrid();
    DrawCaveMesh();
}


void Update() {
    if (Input.GetKeyDown(KeyCode.G)) {
        CellularAutomata(false);
        DrawCaveMesh();
    } else if (Input.GetKeyDown(KeyCode.Space)) {
        CellularAutomata(true);
        DrawCaveMesh();
    } else if (Input.GetKeyDown(KeyCode.N)) {
        InitializeRandomGrid();
        DrawCaveMesh();
    }
}
```

The component exposes four attributes to the Inspector. The first two are simply the weight and height of the map expressed as *number of cells*. Then we have the seed of the random generator in case we want to create specific maps (this is especially useful for debugging purposes). In general, though, we want a random map every time we start the game; that's why we have a useRandomSeed property: if it is true, we initialize a random seed. Finally, we have a private bidimensional array to store the map representation.

After the properties specification, we need to initialize the Start and Update callbacks. These functions will simply call the other functions that we will define next. In Update, we can also see the keys we use to control the demo: every time we press *Spacebar*, we run another step of the CA simulation; when we press the *N* key, we initialize a new map.

When we press the *G* key, we run a different rule for the CA (more on this when we set up the CA rules).

We'll now implement the `InitializeRandomGrid` function. This function initializes the map with random dead and alive cells. However, there are two additional tips. First, the function creates a border of walls (alive cells) around the map. This is because maps are usually bounded, and we do not want the players to jump off the map. This border of walls will ensure that the final map will not have caves leading out of the map edges:

```
void InitializeRandomGrid() {
    map = new int[width, height];
    if (useRandomSeed) {
        seed = (int)DateTime.Now.Ticks;
    }

    System.Random randomGen =
      new System.Random(seed.GetHashCode());

    int mapMiddle = (height / 2);

    for (int c = 0; c < width; c++) {
        for (int r = 0; r < height; r++) {
            if (c == 0 || c == width - 1 || r == 0 || r
                == height - 1) {
                map[c, r] = 1;
            } else {
                if (c == mapMiddle) {
                    map[c, r] = 0;
                } else {
                    map[c, r] = (randomGen.Next(0, 100)
                      < 50) ? 1 : 0;
                }
            }
        }
    }
}
```

The second trick is to keep a vertical line of empty spaces (dead cells). That's the purpose of the check on the `mapMiddle` variable. The motivation for this blank line is simple: it empirically gives better results by generating a main connected cave extending over the entire map. You can remove it to get multiple isolated smaller caves or find a different starting pattern that offers a better outcome according to your tastes and use cases. The `InitializeRandomGrid` function initializes something like the image in *Figure 10.5*.

Figure 10.5 – The initial state of the map

Now, we'll look at a small utility function that we use to count the walls around a specific map cell:

```
int GetSurroundingWallCount(int c, int r, int size) {
    int wallCount = 0;
    for (int iX = c - size; iX <= c + size; iX ++) {
        for (int iY = r - size; iY <= r + size; iY ++)
        {
            if (iX != c || iY != r) {
                wallCount += isWall(iX, iY) ? 1 : 0;
            }
        }
    }
    return wallCount;
}

bool isWall(int c, int r) {
    if (c < 0 || r < 0) {
        return true;
    }
    if (c > width - 1 || r > height - 1) {
        return true;
```

```
        }
        return map[c, r] == 1;
    }
```

The first function is straightforward. It looks at the cells around the target coordinates and counts the number of walls. It also takes a `size` parameter indicating the *radius* around the target coordinate. If `size` is equal to `1`, we check the eight cells around the target coordinates (imagine a 3x3 square). If `size` is equal to `2`, we also check the neighbors' neighbors (imagine a 5x5 square).

The `isWall` function is used to check if a specific coordinate represents a wall. You may ask: why don't we just check the value of map at `(c,r)`? Because we may enter coordinates outside the array (for instance, `(-1, -1)`). In that case, we assume that every cell outside the map is a wall (and it will remain a wall). This simplifies the logic for `GetSurroundingWallCount`.

Now it is time to get to the meat – the CA rules:

```
void CellularAutomata(bool clean = false) {
    int[,] newmap = new int[width, height];
    for (int c = 0; c < width; c ++) {
        for (int r = 0; r < height; r ++) {
            int numWalls =
                GetSurroundingWallCount(c, r, 1);
            int numWalls2 =
                GetSurroundingWallCount(c, r, 2);

            if (isWall(c,r)) {
                if (numWalls > 3) {
                    newmap[c, r] = 1;
                } else {
                    newmap[c, r] = 0;
                }
            } else {
                if (!clean) {
                    if (numWalls >= 5 || numWalls2 <=
                        2) {
                        newmap[c, r] = 1;
                    } else {
```

```
                            newmap[c, r] = 0;
                }
        } else {
                if (numWalls >= 5) {
                        newmap[c, r] = 1;
                } else {
                        newmap[c, r] = 0;
                }
            }
        }
    }
    map = newmap;
}
```

For the cave generator, we use two sets of rules. The first set (obtained when `clean` is equal to `true`) is described as follows:

- If a cell is a wall, it remains a wall as long as it has more than three neighboring walls. Otherwise, it becomes an empty space.

- If a cell is empty, it remains empty as long as it has fewer than five neighboring walls. Otherwise, it becomes a wall.

The second set of rules is identical to the first, but it also checks the neighbors of radius 2. If too many empty spaces surround an empty cell, then it becomes a wall. This optional behavior removes large empty spaces, promoting more narrow passages. However, this can also leave isolated 1x1 walls that look like noise (which is why this set of rules is enabled with the `clean` parameter equal to `false`).

By running these rules, we get maps such as the one in *Figure 10.6*.

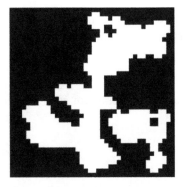

Figure 10.6 – A random cave generated by our algorithm

We now have a perfectly working algorithm but no way to show it in the game. For this, we have the `DrawCaveMesh` function:

```
void DrawCaveMesh() {
    MeshGenerator meshGen =
        GetComponent<MeshGenerator>();
    meshGen.GenerateMesh(map, 1);
}
```

This function simply invokes a mesh generator. We will implement `MeshGenerator` in the next section.

Rendering the generated cave

Given the abstract map representation (the bidimensional array stored in `map`), we need something that converts it into a mesh rendered on screen. We can do this in multiple ways. To allow flexibility, we start by defining an abstract component:

```
using UnityEngine;

public abstract class MeshGenerator : MonoBehaviour {
    abstract public void GenerateMesh(int[,] map, float
                                      squareSize);
}
```

This simple abstract class tells Unity that every valid `MeshGenerator` should contain a `GenerateMesh` function. This function takes as input the array map and the size of each cell expressed in Unity units.

That's cool, but obviously not very useful right now. We still cannot render anything. Do not worry; we will now implement a simple mesh renderer.

Basic mesh renderer

The idea of this renderer is to spawn a 1x1 cube for each wall cell. We'll call this renderer WallGenerator:

```
public class WallGenerator : MeshGenerator {
    public GameObject wallCube;

    public override void GenerateMesh(int[,] map,
      float squareSize) {
        foreach (Transform t in transform) {
            Destroy(t.gameObject);
        }
        int width = map.GetLength(0);
        int height = map.GetLength(1);
        for (int c = 0; c < width; c++) {
            for (int r = 0; r < height; r++) {
                if (map[c, r] == 1) {
                    GameObject obj = Instantiate(wallCube,
                        new Vector3(c * squareSize, 0, r *
                        squareSize), Quaternion.identity);
                    obj.transform.parent = transform;
                }
            }
        }
        transform.position =
          new Vector3(-width / 2.0f, 0, -height / 2.0f);
        MergeCubes();
    }
```

First of all, note that this class extends our abstract MeshGenerator class. Second, this component exposes a single parameter called wallCube. This parameter contains a reference to a wall prefab (basically a colored 3D cube).

Then, we implement the `GenerateMesh` function. The implementation is once again straightforward:

1. We destroy all the existing walls (stored as children).

2. Then, we iterate over every cell in the abstract map and spawn a `wallCube` object in the proper location.

3. We shift the map by half the size (for visualization purposes).

There is a problem, though. Unity is not suitable for spawning thousands of GameObjects. So, if our map is 200x200, this function will potentially spawn 40,000 GameObjects just for rendering the map. The result will be a pretty slow game (and we are not even spawning characters yet).

Fortunately, there is a quick solution:

```
private void MergeCubes() {
    transform.GetComponent<MeshFilter>().mesh =
        new Mesh();
    MeshFilter[] meshFilters =
        GetComponentsInChildren<MeshFilter>();
    CombineInstance[] combine =
        new CombineInstance[meshFilters.Length];

    int i = 0;
    while (i < meshFilters.Length) {
        combine[i].mesh = meshFilters[i].sharedMesh;
        combine[i].transform =
            meshFilters[i].transform.localToWorldMatrix;
        meshFilters[i].gameObject.SetActive(false);

        i++;
    }
    transform.GetComponent<MeshFilter>().mesh =
        new Mesh();
    transform.GetComponent<MeshFilter>()
        .mesh.indexFormat =
        UnityEngine.Rendering.IndexFormat.UInt32;
    transform.GetComponent<MeshFilter>()
```

```
            .mesh.CombineMeshes(combine, true);
        transform.gameObject.SetActive(true);
        foreach (Transform t in ransform) {
            Destroy(t.gameObject);
        }
    }
}
```

The `MergeCubes` function takes all the cubic children we just spawned and combines them in a single game object with a single mesh. We do that by leveraging the built-in `CombineMeshes` tool.

As you can see in the preceding code, we first get all the children (all the individual walls). Then, for each one of them, we create `CombineInstance`. The only tricky thing to remember is to store the coordinates of the mesh in world coordinates (Unity does that by calling `.transform.localToWorldMatrix`).

Once we have all the `CombineInstance` objects, we replace the map's mesh with the mesh obtained by combining all the walls.

Info

Depending on the size of the map, the default mesh `IndexFormat` may be unable to contain all the vertices of the combined mesh. We can solve this by using 32-bit indexing with `transform. GetComponent<MeshFilter>().mesh.indexFormat = UnityEngine.Rendering.IndexFormat.UInt32;`.

Finally, we destroy all the children.

Now we can set up the scene. The final outcome is shown in the following screenshot.

Figure 10.7 – The CaveGen Hierarchy

First, let's create a big plane to use for the ground level, and then an object called `CaveGen`. The `CaveGen` object contains a `MeshRenderer` and a `MeshFilter` component (but no mesh).

Now attach the `CaveGenerator` and `WallRenderer` components to this object and configure them as in the following screenshot.

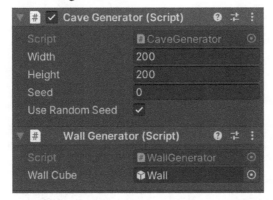

Figure 10.8 – The CaveGenerator and WallGenerator components

The final touch is adding a **Wall** prefab to **Wall Cube**. Then, finally, we can click **Play**, and we should see something similar to *Figure 10.9*.

Figure 10.9 – The initial random configuration

We can now continue the map generation by pressing *Spacebar* (or *G* if we want to apply the second set of CA rules). After some time, you may note that the map stabilizes into a map like the one in *Figure 10.10*. At that point, your map is ready (but you can start over by pressing *N*).

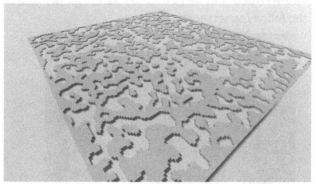

Figure 10.10 – The completely evolved map

Not bad for a PCG algorithm that we wrote in less than 130 lines of code.

Advanced mesh renderer

`WallGenerator` is quick and effective; however, it is not optimal. The final mesh contains a lot of redundant vertices, and we still have this pixelated look. There are many other different algorithms that we can use to generate a mesh. A standard solution is to use the **Marching Squares** algorithm (also called **Marching Cubes** if applied to 3D).

This algorithm is a bit complex, and a detailed discussion would go way beyond the scope of this book. However, in the code of this demo, I've included a `MarchingCubesGenerator` component for you to use and explore. The algorithm is taken from an official Unity tutorial (`https://www.youtube.com/watch?v=yOgIncKp0BE`) and I have adapted it for this demo.

To use it, you just need to replace the `WallGenerator` component with `MarchingCubesGenerator`. If you now run the game and run the CA for a couple of generations, you should see something like *Figure 10.11*.

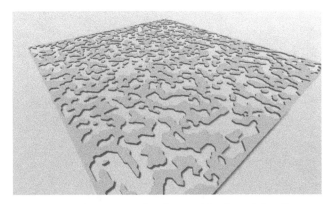

Figure 10.11 – The map rendered using MarchingCubesGenerator

As you can see, we get smoother walls and much fewer vertices (with improved performance). If you like this cave generator and want to explore it in depth, I encourage you to go to the official tutorial by navigating to `https://learn.unity.com/tutorial/generating-content`.

Summary

In this chapter, we barely scratched the surface of PCG. First, we started with a simple algorithm to create randomized goblin biographies. Then, we unleashed the power of CA to develop an intricate cave system and discovered two techniques to render abstract grids in 3D maps.

However, as I said, this is just the beginning. PCG represents a massive class of algorithms blending the boundary between programming and art. PCG alone is a programming field worth exploring, and this short chapter's goal was to give you just a tiny taste of it.

Now, though, we have no more time for PCG. It is time to move on to machine learning in the next chapter.

Further reading

If you are interested in a deeper exploration of PCG in Unity, Ryan Watkins wrote an entire book on the topic titled *Procedural Content Generation for Unity Game Development* for *Packt*.

11
Machine Learning in Unity

Machine learning is the hottest buzzword in **Artificial Intelligence** (**AI**). Nowadays, everything contains (or claims to contain) some machine learning-powered AI that is supposed to improve our life: calendars, to-do apps, photo management software, every smartphone, and much more. However, even if the phrase *machine learning* is just a marketing gimmick most of the time, it is without question that machine learning has improved significantly in recent years. Most importantly, though, there are now plenty of tools that allow everybody to implement a learning algorithm without any previous academic-level AI knowledge.

At the moment, machine learning is not used in game development (except for applications for procedural content generation). There are many reasons for that. The main reason, though, is that a designer can't control the output of a machine learning agent, and in game design, uncontrollable outcomes often correlate to not-fun games. For this reason, game AI developers prefer more predictable and straightforward techniques, such as behavior trees.

On the other hand, being able to use machine learning algorithms in Unity is useful for non-gaming purposes, such as simulations, AI research, and *some serious* gaming applications. Whatever the reason, Unity provides a complete toolkit for machine learning that spares us the complication of interfacing the game engine with an external machine learning framework.

In this chapter, we will look at the following topics:

- An introduction to the Unity Machine Learning Agents Toolkit
- Setting up the Unity Machine Learning Agents Toolkit
- Seeing how to run a simple example

Machine learning is an extensive topic; therefore, we do not expect to cover every single aspect of it. Instead, look at the toolkit documentation and the additional resources linked at the end of this chapter for further reference.

Technical requirements

For this chapter, you need Unity3D 2022, Python 3.7, PyTorch, and the ML-Agents Toolkit installed on your system. Don't worry if you don't; we will go over the installation steps. You can find the example project described in this chapter in the `Chapter 11` folder in the book's repository: `https://github.com/PacktPublishing/Unity-Artificial-Intelligence-Programming-Fifth-Edition/tree/main/Chapter11`

The Unity Machine Learning Agents Toolkit

The **Unity Machine Learning Agents Toolkit** (**ML-Agents Toolkit**) is a collection of software and plugins that help developers write autonomous game agents powered by machine learning algorithms. You can explore and download the source code at the GitHub repository at `https://github.com/Unity-Technologies/ml-agents`.

The ML-Agents Toolkit is based on the reinforcement learning algorithm. Simplistically, reinforcement learning is the algorithmic equivalent of training a dog. For example, if you want to teach a dog some trick, you give him a command, and then, when the dog does what you expect, you reward him. The reward tells your dog that it responded correctly to the command, and therefore, the next time it hears the same command, it will do the same thing to get a new reward.

> **Note**
> In reinforcement learning, you can also punish your agent when doing the wrong things, but in the dog-training example, I can assure you that punishment is entirely unnecessary. Just give them rewards!

For an AI agent trained with reinforcement learning, we perform a similar cycle:

1. When an agent acts, the action influences the world (such as changing the Agent's position, moving an object around, collecting a coin, gaining score points, and so on).

2. The algorithm then sends the new world state back to the Agent with a reward (or punishment).

3. When the Agent decides its following action, it will choose the action that maximizes the expected reward (or minimizes the expected punishment).

For this reason, it is clear that training a reinforcement learning agent requires several simulations of the scenario in which the Agent acts, receives a reward, updates its decision-making values, performs another action, and so on. This work is offloaded from Unity to Torch via PyTorch. **Torch** is a popular open source machine learning library used, among others, by tech giants such as Facebook and IBM.

Refer to the *Further reading* section at the end of the chapter for more information on reinforcement learning.

Let's now see how to install the toolkit.

Installing the ML-Agents Toolkit

As a first step, we need to download the toolkit. We can do this by cloning the repository with the following command:

```
git clone --branch release_19 https://github.com/Unity-
Technologies/ml-agents.git
```

This command creates an `ml-agents` folder in your current folder. The ML-Agents Toolkit is composed of two main components:

*   A Python package containing the Python interface for Unity and PyTorch's trainers (stored in the `ml-agents` folder)

*   A Python package containing the interface with OpenAI Gym (`https://gym.openai.com/`), a toolkit for training reinforcement learning agents (stored in the `gym-unity` folder).

> **Information**
>
> **Git** is the most famous version-control application in the world. It is used to store your source code, keep track of different versions, collaborate with other people, and much more. If you are not already using Git, you should really check it out. You can download it from `https://git-scm.com/`.

Now, it is time to install the required dependencies.

Installing Python and PyTorch on Windows

The suggested version of Python for the ML-Agents Toolkit is version 3.7. You can install it in many ways, the faster of which is by searching in Microsoft Store for Python 3.7 (or follow this link: `https://www.microsoft.com/en-us/p/python-37/9nj46sx7x90p`).

On Windows, you need to manually install PyTorch before installing the `mlagents` package. To do that, you can simply run this command in a terminal:

```
pip3 install torch~=1.7.1 -f https://download.pytorch.org/whl/
torch_stable.html
```

> **Information**
>
> If you have any difficulties installing PyTorch, you can refer to the official installation guide at `https://pytorch.org/get-started/locally/`.

After this step, you should be able to follow the same installation steps for macOS and Unix-like systems.

Installing Python and PyTorch on macOS and Unix-like systems

To install the ML-Agents Toolkit on macOS or Linux, you need first to install Python 3.6 or Python 3.7 (at the moment, the ML-Agents Toolkit recommends only these two Python versions).

Then, you can run the following command:

```
python -m pip install mlagents==0.28.0
```

On macOS and Linux, this command installs automatically the correct version of PyTorch.

After the installation, if everything is correct, you should be able to run the `mlagents-learn --help` command without any errors from any place in the system.

> **Note**
> Pip3 is automatically installed with any Python 3.x distribution. If, for some reason, you don't have `pip3` installed, try following the official guide: `https://pip.pypa.io/en/latest/installing/`.

Using the ML-Agents Toolkit – a basic example

Now that everything is installed, we can start using the ML-Agents Toolkit. First, let's explain the basic architecture of an ML-Agents scene.

An ML-Agents scene is called a **learning environment**. The learning environment is a standard Unity scene and contains two main elements:

- **The agent**: Obviously, the Agent is the central object in the ML-Agents Toolkit. An agent is an object that performs an action, receives information from the environment, and can receive rewards for actions. To create an Agent, you need to subclass the `Agent` class and write the behavior for the agent. For instance, if the Agent is a car, we need to write how the car is controlled by the input and how we can reward and penalize the car (for example, we can reward the vehicle for going above a certain speed and punish it when it goes off-road). A learning environment can have as many agents as you like.

- **The academy**: This component is a singleton (therefore, it doesn't need to be explicitly instantiated in the scene in a game object) that orchestrates the agents in the scene and is responsible for their training and decision making. Each sequence of actions and data collection is called an **episode**. An episode usually starts from a default starting configuration and ends when the Agent performs a maximum number of steps, reaches a goal, or fails to reach a goal. In particular, for every episode, the academy does the following operations:

  - Invokes `OnEpisodeBegin()` for each `Agent` in the scene.

  - Invokes `CollectObservations(VectorSensor sensor)` for each `Agent` in the scene. This function is used to collect information on the environment so that each `Agent` can update its internal model.

  - Invokes `OnActionReceived()` for every `Agent` in the scene. This function executes the action chosen by each `Agent` and collects the rewards (or penalty).

  - If an agent completes its episode, the academy calls `OnEpisodeBegin()` for the Agent. This function is responsible for resetting the Agent in the starting configuration.

To start using the ML-Agents Toolkit, we need to do the following:

1. Open Unity and create an empty project.
2. Go to **Windows | Package Manager**.
3. In the top-left menu, select **Unity Registry**:

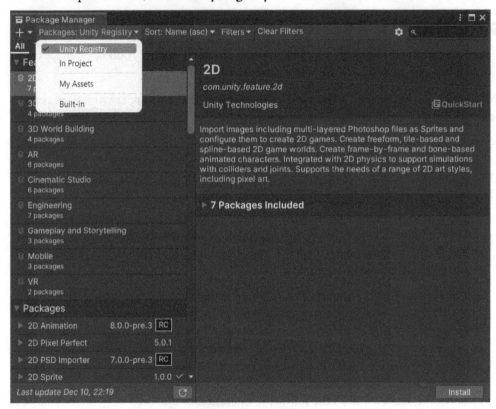

Figure 11.1 – The Unity Package Manager

4.   Look for the **ML Agents** package and install it:

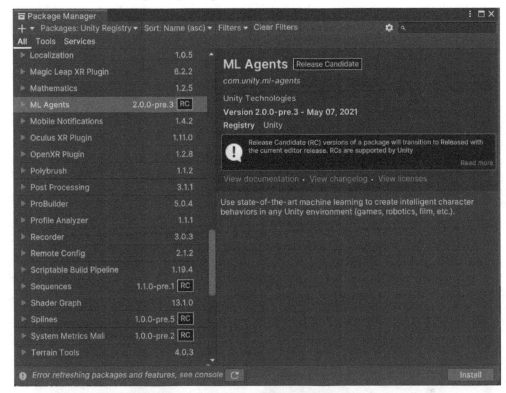

Figure 11.2 – The ML Agents package in Package Manager

We need to make sure that we are using the correct runtime.

5. To do so, go to **Edit | Project Settings | Player**, and for each platform (PC, Mac, Android, and so on), go into **Other Settings** and make sure that **Api Compatibility Level** is set to **.NET Framework**. If not, adjust these settings to be as we need them and then save, as follows:

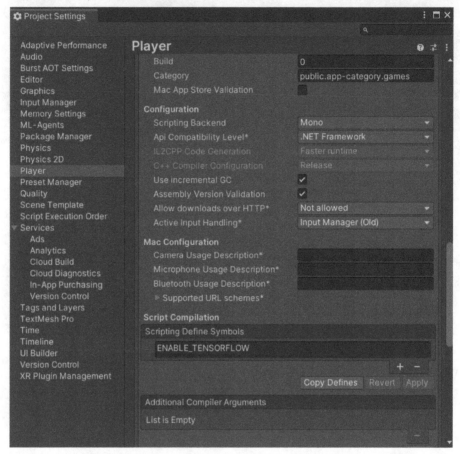

Figure 11.3 – The Project Settings window with the correct settings

Creating the scene

Creating a learning environment is easy. Let's create a simple 3D scene with a plane, a sphere, and a cube, as shown in the following screenshot:

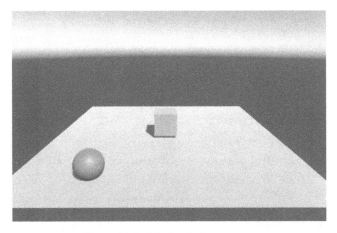

Figure 11.4 – The basic demo scene

We put the cube at the plane's center and add a `Rigidbody` component to the sphere. This scene aims to train a rolling ball to reach the target (the cube) without falling from the plane.

Implementing the code

Now, we need to implement the code that will describe the Agent's behavior and the ML-Agent's academy. The agent's behavior script describes how the Agents perform actions in the simulation, the reward the Agent receives, and how we reset it to start a new simulation:

1. Select the sphere. Let's add to it a new script, called `SphereAgent`, with the following content:

```
using System.Collections.Generic;
using UnityEngine;
using Unity.MLAgents;
using Unity.MLAgents.Sensors;
using Unity.MLAgents.Actuators;

public class SphereAgent : Agent {
    Rigidbody rBody;
    public Transform Target;
    public float forceMultiplier = 10;

    void Start () {
```

```
        rBody = GetComponent<Rigidbody>();
    }


    override public void OnEpisodeBegin() {
        if (transform.position.y < -1.0) {
            // The agent fell
            transform.position = Vector3.zero;
            rBody.angularVelocity = Vector3.zero;
            rBody.velocity = Vector3.zero;
        } else {
            // Move the target to a new spot
            Target.position = new Vector3(Random.value *
                8 - 4, 0.5f, Random.value * 8 - 4);
        }
    }
}
```

This is the base agent for our demo. `OnEpisodeBegin` is a function called by the system every time we want to reset the training scene. In our example, we check whether the sphere fell from the plane and bring it back to zero; otherwise, we move it to a random location.

2. We need to add the `CollectObservations` method to `SphereAgent`. The agent uses this method to get information from the game world and then uses it to perform a decision:

```
    override public void CollectObservations(
       VectorSensor sensor) {
        // Calculate relative position
        Vector3 relativePosition =
          Target.position - transform.position;
        // Relative position
        sensor.AddObservation(relativePosition.x/5);
        sensor.AddObservation(relativePosition.z / 5);
        // Distance to edges of platform
        sensor.AddObservation(
```

```
        (transform.position.x + 5) / 5);
    sensor.AddObservation(
      (transform.position.x - 5) / 5);
    sensor.AddObservation(
      (transform.position.z + 5) / 5);
    sensor.AddObservation(
      (transform.position.z - 5) / 5);
    // agent velocity
    sensor.AddObservation(rBody.velocity.x / 5);
    sensor.AddObservation(rBody.velocity.z / 5);      }
```

In this example, we are interested in the following:

- The relative position of the sphere agent from the cube (the target). We are only interested in the x and z values because the sphere only moves on the plane (note that we normalize the values by dividing by 5, which is half the default plane size).

- The distance from the plane's edges.

- The sphere's velocity.

3. We need to implement the `OnActionReceived` method. This method is called whenever the Agent needs to act. The method takes a single parameter of the `ActionBuffer` type. The `ActionBuffer` object contains a description of the control inputs for the sphere. In our case, we only need two continuous actions, corresponding to the force applied along the x and z axes of the game.

4. We also need to define the rewards. As said before, we reward the Agent with one point by calling `SetReward` when we reach the target. If the Agent falls off the plane, we end the episode with zero points by calling `EndEpisode`. The final version of the code is the following:

```
    public override void OnActionReceived(
      ActionBuffers actionBuffers) {
        // Actions, size = 2
        Vector3 controlSignal = Vector3.zero;
        controlSignal.x =
          actionBuffers.ContinuousActions[0];
        controlSignal.z =
          actionBuffers.ContinuousActions[1];
```

```
        rBody.AddForce(controlSignal * forceMultiplier);

        // Rewards
        float distanceToTarget = Vector3.Distance(this.
            transform.localPosition, Target.localPosition);

        // Reached target
        if (distanceToTarget < 1.42f) {
            SetReward(1.0f);
            EndEpisode();
        }

        // Fell off platform
        else if (this.transform.localPosition.y < 0) {
            EndEpisode();
        }
    }}
```

Now, it is time to connect this `SphereAgent` script to our sphere.

Adding the final touches

Now, we need to connect all the pieces to make the demo work:

1. First, we attach the `SphereAgent` script to the sphere.
2. We drag and drop the cube into the **Target** field of the **Sphere Agent** component.
3. We add a **Decision Requester** component by clicking on **Add Component**. We can leave the default settings.
4. In the **Behavior Parameters** script, we set up `MovingSphere`.
5. We set the **Vector Observation | Space Size** value to 8, corresponding to the number of observations we added in the `CollectObservations` method.

6. Finally, we set the **Actions | Continuous Actions** value to 2. At this point, the sphere scripts should look like the following screenshot:

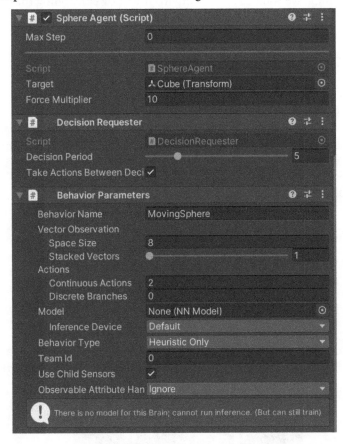

Figure 11.5 – The Inspector view for the sphere agent

It is now to test our environment.

Testing the learning environment

Before we start learning, we want to test the environment by controlling the Agents with manual input. It is very useful to debug the learning environment without wasting hours of the training process.

Fortunately, the ML-Agents Toolkit makes it very handy to control an agent with live input. We only need two steps:

1. We add the `Heuristic` method to the `SphereAgent` component. This function allows us to manually specify the values of the `ActionBuffer` objects. In our case, we want to add the two continuous actions to the input axes of the controller:

```
public override void Heuristic(
  in ActionBuffers actionsOut) {
    var continuousActionsOut =
      actionsOut.ContinuousActions;
    continuousActionsOut[0] =
      Input.GetAxis("Horizontal");
    continuousActionsOut[1] =
      Input.GetAxis("Vertical");
}
```

2. Now, we go to the Inspector and set the **Behavior Type** parameter to **Heuristic Only**:

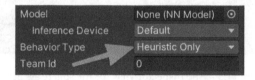

Figure 11.6 – The Behavior Type configuration

At this point, you can press **Play** in Unity, and you should be able to control the sphere using the arrow key (or a gaming controller stick). You can test the environment by checking the episode's behavior. If you reach the target cube, it should disappear and spawn in another random location. If you fall from the plane, you should respawn on the plane.

If everything looks fine, it is time to train the Agent automatically.

Training an agent

Before we can start training, we need to write a training configuration file. Open your terminal and go into any empty folder. Then, create a `sphere.yaml` file with the following code:

```yaml
behaviors:
  MovingSphere:
    trainer_type: ppo
    hyperparameters:
      batch_size: 10
      buffer_size: 100
      learning_rate: 3.0e-4
      beta: 5.0e-4
      epsilon: 0.2
      lambd: 0.99
      num_epoch: 3
      learning_rate_schedule: linear
      beta_schedule: constant
      epsilon_schedule: linear
    network_settings:
      normalize: false
      hidden_units: 128
      num_layers: 2
    reward_signals:
      extrinsic:
        gamma: 0.99
        strength: 1.0
    max_steps: 500000
    time_horizon: 64
    summary_freq: 10000
```

Then, we need to be sure to change the **Behavior Type** parameter in the sphere object to **Default**.

Now, from the same folder, we should be able to run the following command:

```
mlagents-learn sphere.yaml --run-id=myMovingSphere
```

run-id is a unique ID for your running session. If everything is going according to plan, you should see the **Start training by pressing the Play button in the Unity Editor** message on the terminal window at some point. Now, you can do as the message says and press **Play** in Unity.

After the training is complete, you will find the trained model in the results/ myMovingSphere/MovingSphere.onnx file (the results folder inside the folder, in which you run the mlagents-learn command).

Copy this file inside your Unity project and then put this in the **Model** placeholder in the **Behavior Parameters** component of the sphere:

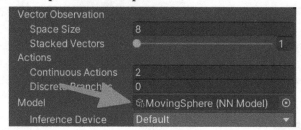

Figure 11.7 – The trained MovingSphere model inside the behavior parameters

Now, if you press **Play**, the Sphere will move autonomously according to the training model. It is not something big and complex, but it is automated learning nevertheless.

Summary

In this chapter, we barely scratched the surface of machine learning and how to use it for training Unity agents. We learned how to install Unity's official ML-Agents Toolkit, set up a learning environment, and trained the model. However, this is just a basic introduction to the ML-Agents Toolkit, and many unexplored directions are waiting for you. I encourage you to look at the ML-Agents official repository; it includes many interesting demo projects.

In the next chapter, we will wrap everything up by developing an AI agent into a more complex game demo.

Further reading

- For more information, I encourage you to check the in-depth documentation for ML-Agents in the official repository (`https://github.com/Unity-Technologies/ml-agents/tree/master/docs`).

- For a more in-depth (but still very accessible) introduction to reinforcement learning, there is a good article on freeCodeCamp (`https://medium.freecodecamp.org/an-introduction-to-reinforcement-learning-4339519de419`).

- If you are willing to go even deeper into reinforcement learning, a perfect next step is *Deep Reinforcement Learning Hands-On, Second Edition, Maxim Lapan, Packt Publishing.*

12
Putting It All Together

Over the previous eleven chapters, we've looked at various AI methods and built some simple demo applications using Unity3D. In this final chapter, we'll develop a more complex game example using some of the techniques we explored in previous chapters. The techniques we'll be using in this chapter include navigation meshes and **finite-state machines (FSMs)**, but, more importantly, we will learn how to navigate and add AI to a pre-existing complex game. So, unlike the other chapters, this example is more like a real-world scenario.

In this chapter, we'll add AI to a simple tank combat game called *TANKS!* and contained in one of the official Unity tutorials, which, in turn, was inspired by an historic tank game called *Combat* for the Atari 2600. In the default version, TANKS! is a two-player game. Each player takes control of a tank, and the goal is to destroy each other. To make things more complicated, the player can decide the shot's strength (and, thus, the distance) by pressing and holding the *Spacebar* for a shorter or longer duration.

However, because we are AI developers, we want to build an AI for the enemy tank to play in single-player mode. So, this is what we'll do in this chapter.

In this chapter, we will cover the following topics:

- Developing the basic game structure
- Adding automated navigation
- Creating decision-making AI with FSM

Technical requirements

For this chapter, you just need Unity3D 2022. You can find the example project described in this chapter in the `Chapter 12` folder in the book's GitHub repository: `https://github.com/PacktPublishing/Unity-Artificial-Intelligence-Programming-Fifth-Edition/tree/main/Chapter12`.

Developing the basic game structure

For this demo, we will write an AI for the free tutorial game *TANKS!*. You can download the base game from Unity Asset Store (`https://assetstore.unity.com/packages/essentials/tutorial-projects/tanks-tutorial-46209`), or follow along with the version included in the `Chapter 12` folder of this book's GitHub repository. The version included with this book has the advantage of already having been tested for Unity 2022.

In either case, the game is the same. When we start the game, we see a pleasant desert scenario, with rocks, structures, palm trees, and so on. Using the keyboard, we should be able to control the blue tank (the tank moves with *W*, *A*, *S*, and *D* and shoots with the *Spacebar*).

The following screenshot shows the basic structure of the game:

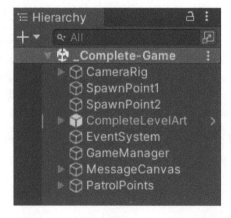

Figure 12.1 – Basic hierarchy of the game

The first time you start with an existing project, spend as much time as you can familiarizing yourself with the game structure, the basic scripts, and the components. You must know how to operate at ease in a project you don't know. To do this, run the game a couple of times, try minor modifications to the code to see the effect, and add debug messages to learn about the flow in which information moves around the game. The following image will give you an idea of how the game will look when we run it:

Figure 12.2 – The TANKS! game in action

> **Info**
>
> It may be helpful to follow the complete Unity tutorial, available at `https://unity3d.com/learn/tutorials/s/tanks-tutorial`. Even if it does not involve AI and is quite old (the tutorial has been recorded in 2015), you will still find many important teachings for game development, such as how to design a game manager, basic controls, and audio.

Adding automated navigation

The first step is to modify the level to support automated navigation. In the original game, the players control all the moving objects (the tanks), so pathfinding is unnecessary. Now that we want to add AI, we need to have a world representation through which the AI can move. Luckily, this process is straightforward, thanks to NavMeshes.

Creating the NavMesh

To do this, perform the following steps:

1. Open the Navigation window (**Window | AI | Navigation**) and look at the NavMesh generation parameters. In this case, NavMesh generation is relatively easy: we are only interested in moving around on the ground surface plane, so there are no jumps, no links, and no slopes we need to care of.

2. The only adjustment to the default NavMesh parameters we need to make is for the baking agent size (that is, the measures of the virtual agent used by Unity to verify whether a location is large enough to allow the Agent to pass).

3. The tanks used in the game are about three units large, so we need to instruct the generator to remove the areas that are too small for the tank to pass through. The following screenshot shows the baking setting for the navigation mesh:

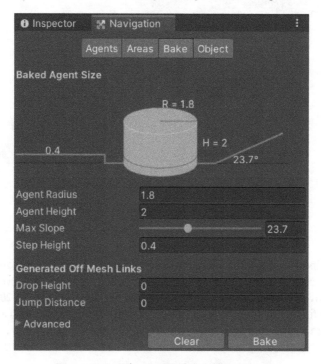

Figure 12.3 – The NavMesh baking options

Just to be on the safe side, we use an **Agent Radius** value of 1.8 and reduce the **Max Slope** value to about 20 (after all, we are not interested in slopes: the game is completely flat).

4. After that, press **Bake**. You should get a nice NavMesh, as in the following screenshot:

Figure 12.4 – The baked NavMesh in the map

5. We now want to add some patrolling points that the AI tank can follow. To do this, we create an empty GameObject; feel free to create as many other GameObject instances as you like.

6. Then, we create a `PatrolPoint` tag, and tag all the patrol points with it.

Figure 12.5 – The patrol points labeled PPoint in the Editor view

Now that we have a world representation and a set of points that we can use to wander around, we need to create an AI-controlled agent.

Setting up the Agent

Unfortunately, the game does not support AI, so we need to add the Agent ourselves. To do this, perform the following steps:

1. We have to identify the player tank. There is no tank in the scene, as you can see from the game hierarchy. As you should know from your preliminary exploration, it is the job of `GameManager` to spawn the tanks. The tank model we'll use is a prefab called **CompleteTank**.

2. Let's copy the prefab and call it `CompleteTankAI`.

3. Then we need to add the **Nav Mesh Agent** component to it so that we can move it around on the new NavMesh.

Figure 12.6 – The Inspector for the Nav Mesh Agent component

But this is not enough. First, we'll reuse the `TankShooting` script from the **TANKS!** demo, so we need to disable shooting if this script is attached to an AI (otherwise, the player could shoot for the AI agent).

4. For this, we create a public Boolean variable, called `m_IsAI`. Note that for this demo, we are using the variable naming convention of the original tutorial. This is to not confuse people working from the Asset Store. Moreover, it is always wise to adopt the coding convention of an existing project without imposing our preferences on the entire code base. Anyway, let's add the following lines to the `Update` script:

```
private void Update () {
    if (m_IsAI) {
        return;
    }
    ...
```

These lines just stop the `Update` script for the AI agent, thereby disabling player input for AI characters. It is important to enable this variable in the AI tank prefab. We also need to add another patch; in fact, if we disable the input, we will also disable the shot strength.

5. So, we need to add this back into the `Fire` function:

```
// We need to make Fire public.
public void Fire (){
    // Set the fired flag so only Fire is only called
    // once.
    m_Fired = true;

    // Create an instance of the shell and store a
    // reference to its rigidbody.
    Rigidbody shellInstance = Instantiate (m_Shell,
        m_FireTransform.position,
        m_FireTransform.rotation) as Rigidbody;

    // New lines: if AI, we shoot with average force.
    if (m_IsAI) {
        m_CurrentLaunchForce =
            m_MaxLaunchForce / 2.0f;
    }
    // Set the shell's velocity to the launch force in
    // the fire position's forward direction.
```

```
        shellInstance.velocity =
          m_CurrentLaunchForce * m_FireTransform.forward;


        // Change the clip to the firing clip and play it.
        m_ShootingAudio.clip = m_FireClip;
        m_ShootingAudio.Play ();


        // Reset the launch force. This is a precaution in
        // case of missing button events.
        m_CurrentLaunchForce = m_MinLaunchForce;
    }
```

We are replacing the variable shooting force with a constant shooting force for simplicity.

> **Info**
>
> As an exercise, you could make m_CurrentLaunchForce a parameter of the Fire () functions. We also make the Fire () function public: in fact, we need to call this function from the FSM that we'll implement later.

Finally, we can remove the TankMovement component from the Tank AI prefab. Now it is time to update the GameManager script to enable *player versus computer* mode.

Fixing the GameManager script

As a final step, we need to instruct the GameManager script to spawn a player tank and an AI tank:

1. Open the GameManager script and add a new public variable in which we'll store the new AI tank prefab:

    ```
    // Reference to the prefab the players will control.
    public GameObject m_TankPrefab;
    // Reference to the prefab the AI will control.
    public GameObject m_TankAIPrefab;
    ```

2. Then, modify the SpawnAllTanks function in this way:

    ```
    private void SpawnAllTanks(){
        // Spaw the Player
        m_Tanks[0].m_Instance = Instantiate(m_TankPrefab,
    ```

```
                m_Tanks[0].m_SpawnPoint.position,
                m_Tanks[0].m_SpawnPoint.rotation);
        m_Tanks[0].m_PlayerNumber = 01;
        m_Tanks[0].Setup();

        // Spawn the AI Tanks
        for (int i = 1; i < m_Tanks.Length; i++) {
            m_Tanks[i].m_Instance =
                Instantiate(m_TankAIPrefab,
                m_Tanks[i].m_SpawnPoint.position,
                m_Tanks[i].m_SpawnPoint.rotation);
            m_Tanks[i].m_PlayerNumber = i + 1;
            m_Tanks[i].Setup();
        }
    }
```

Now that this game is a single-player game, we assume that the first tank is always the player (we spawn the m_TankPrefab model), and any other tank is AI-controlled (we spawn the m_TankAIPrefab model).

3. Finally, just add the prefab to the Inspector as follows. Remember to enable the m_IsAI variable in the CompleteTankAI prefab and change its layer from **Player** to **AI**.

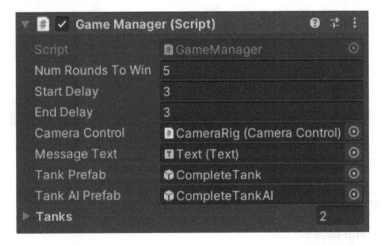

Figure 12.7 – The Game Manager script in the inspector

Now that we have set up the basics, it is finally time to write the AI of the enemy tanks.

Creating decision-making AI with FSM

In *Chapter 2*, *Finite State Machines*, we saw how to implement a simple FSM. In this section, we are using the same technique, but will apply it to the more complex scenario of this demo.

First, we need an FSM plan. We are interested only in connecting the FSM to the existing game for this demo, so we will keep it simple. The FSM for our tank is composed of just two states – patrolling and shooting.

The plan is nice and straightforward:

1. The AI tank starts in the `Patrol` state and wanders around the previously defined patrolling points.
2. Then, if the players get in range, the tank switches to the `Attack` state.
3. In the `Attack` state, the tank turns toward the player and starts shooting at it.
4. Finally, if we are in the `Attack` state and the players leave the AI's range, the tank will return to the `Patrol` state.

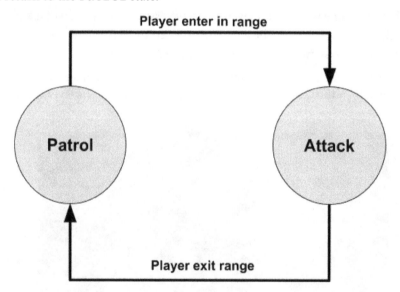

Figure 12.8 – The simple FSM for the enemy tanks

For the implementation, perform the following steps:

1. Let's start with the FSM class:

    ```
    using UnityEngine;
    using System.Collections;
    ```

```
public class FSM : Complete.TankMovement {
    // Next destination position of the NPC Tank
    protected Vector3 destPos;

    // List of points for patrolling
    protected GameObject[] pointList;

    protected virtual void Initialize() { }
    protected virtual void FSMUpdate() { }
    protected virtual void FSMFixedUpdate() { }

    // Use this for initialization
    void Start() {
        Initialize();
    }

    // Update is called once per frame
    void Update() {
        FSMUpdate();
    }

    void FixedUpdate() {
        FSMFixedUpdate();
    }
}
```

As you can see, this class extends the `Complete.TankMovement` script. In this way, we can reuse the existing `TankMovement` code for things such as the engine sounds and other cosmetic aspects.

As explained in *Chapter 2, Finite State Machines*, the FSM class stores the data we need for the decision-making AI. Moreover, it contains the functions that the actual **Tank Controller** can override for the `Update`, `FixedUpdate`, and `Start` methods. In the FSM class, we want to store all the patrol points and the destination point (the current patrol points the tank is looking for).

2. Now it is time for the complete controller. We create a new `AITankController` script with the following initial content:

```
using UnityEngine;
using System;
using UnityEngine.AI;

public class AITankController : FSM {
    public Complete.TankShooting tankShooter;
    public Complete.TankHealth tankHealth;
    public float playerChaseRadius = 15.0f;
    public float platerAttackRadius = 10.0f;
    public float shootRate = 3.0f;
    public float targetReachedRadius = 5.0f;

    private bool isDead = false;
    private float elapsedTime = 0.0f;

    private GameObject player = null;
    private NavMeshAgent navMeshAgent;

    public enum FSMState {
        None, Patrol, Attack, Dead,
    }

    // Current state that the NPC is reaching
    public FSMState curState;
...
```

In the preceding code, the class starts by extending FSM and defining the states. As you can see in the `FSMState` enum, we have `Patrol` and `Attack`, an empty state (`None`), and a final state (`Dead`). Then we add some class attributes to store the data we need.

The first two attributes are references to the `TankShooter` and `TankHealth` scripts in the tank. We will use them to check the health and to fire bullets. Then we have an `isDead` Boolean to stop FSM execution. Then we have `elapsedTime` and `shootRate` for controlling how rapidly the tank will shoot, followed by two private attributes that store a reference to the player (if in range) and a reference to `NavMeshAgent`. Lastly, we have a variable holding the current state in the FSM.

3. The `Initialize` function is used to initialize, of course, the FSM:

```
    //Initialize the Finite state machine for the NPC
tank
    protected override void Initialize() {
        navMeshAgent = GetComponent<NavMeshAgent>();

        // Get the list of points
        pointList = GameObject.FindGameObjectsWithTag(
          "PatrolPoint");

        int rndIndex = UnityEngine.Random.Range(0,
          pointList.Length);
        destPos =
          pointList[rndIndex].transform.position;

    }
```

In this function, we do three things:

- We get the reference to `NavMeshAgent`.
- We get a list of all `PatrolPoint` in the scene
- We randomly select one of the patrol points as the Agent's current destination.

4. Then it is time for the `Update` function. Before this, however, we need to expose the tanks' current health. Let's add the following line to the `TankHealth` component:

```
    // ...
    private AudioSource m_ExplosionAudio
    private ParticleSystem m_ExplosionParticles
    private float m_CurrentHealth;
    private bool m_Dead;
    public float CurrentHealth { get; }
    // ...
```

We add the `CurrentHealth` property so that we can get read-only public access to the private member, `m_CurrentHealth`.

5. We are now ready to implement the FSM's `FSMUpdate` method:

```
protected override void FSMUpdate() {
    switch (curState) {
        case FSMState.Patrol:
            UpdatePatrolState();
            break;
        case FSMState.Attack:
            UpdateAttackState();
            break;
        case FSMState.Dead:
            UpdateDeadState();
            break;
    }

    elapsedTime += Time.deltaTime;

    // Go to dead state is no health left
    if (tankHealth.CurrentHealth <= 0) {
        curState = FSMState.Dead;
    }
}
```

As we explained previously, the main task of the `Update` function is to invoke the proper function depending on the current state. In addition to that, `FSMUpdate` also updates the `elapsedTime` timer and sets the Agent to the `Dead` state if the tank has no health.

6. The `Dead` state is very simple: the tank does nothing, and writes on the console that it is dead:

```
private void UpdateDeadState() {
    if (!isDead) {
        Debug.Log("Dead");
    }
}
```

7. The `Attack` state is more interesting:

```
private void UpdateAttackState() {
```

```
Collider[] players = Physics.OverlapSphere(
   Transform.position, playerChaseRadius,
   LayerMask.GetMask("Players"));
if (players.Length == 0) {
   curState = FSMState.Patrol;
   player = null;
   navMeshAgent.enabled = true;
   return;
}

player = players[0].gameObject;

Vector3 _direction =
   (player.transform.position -
    transform.position).normalized;
Quaternion _lookRotation =
   Quaternion.LookRotation(_direction);
transform.rotation =
   Quaternion.Slerp(transform.rotation,
   _lookRotation, Time.deltaTime * 3);

if (elapsedTime > shootRate) {
   tankShooter.Fire();
   elapsedTime = 0;
}
}
```

In the first part of the preceding code, we cast a sphere using Unity's physics engine to *see* all the *players* in a radius of 15 units. Then, if there is none (meaning that the player is out of range), we switch to the Patrol state, remove the player reference, enable the NavMeshAgent component, and terminate the state. Otherwise, we proceed with the attack: we get the player reference, rotate the tank in its direction, and shoot (at the correct rate).

Luckily, the original game already implemented the Fire function! That's why good class design is essential: if a class is functional, you can reutilize it very well, even for things that you didn't initially consider!

8. Finally, we have the `Patrol` state function:

```
private void UpdatePatrolState() {
    Collider[] players = Physics.OverlapSphere(
        transform.position, playerAttackRadius,
        LayerMask.GetMask("Players")"));

    if (players.Length > 0) {
        curState = FSMState.Attack;
        player = players[0].gameObject;
        navMeshAgent.enabled = false;
        return;
    }

    if (IsInCurrentRange(destPos)) {
        int rndIndex = UnityEngine.Random.Range(0,
            pointList.Length);
        destPos =
            pointList[rndIndex].transform.position;
    }

    navMeshAgent.destination = destPos;
}
```

If no player is in range, then we proceed to wander around. First, we check whether we have reached the current destination. If so, we need to select a new destination. Then, we set up the patrol point as the destination of the `navMeshAgent` component (as described in *Chapter 8*, *Navigation Mesh*).

9. The `IsInCurrentRange` function is just a simple comparison, as shown in the following code:

```
protected bool IsInCurrentRange(Vector3 pos) {
    float xPos =
        Mathf.Abs(pos.x - transform.position.x);
    float zPos =
        Mathf.Abs(pos.z - transform.position.z);

    if (xPos <= targetReachedRadius  && zPos <=
```

```
            targetReachedRadius ) return true;


        return false;
    }
}
```

10. That's it. Add the `AITankController` script to the `CompleteAITank` prefab and connect all the required elements. You can see how the `AITankController` component should look in the following screenshot:

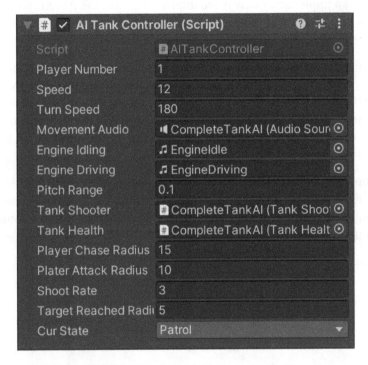

Figure 12.9 – The AI Tank Controller script in the Inspector

Remember also to set the prefab's layer to **AI**.

Figure 12.10 – The Layer configuration for the CompleteTankAI prefab

At this point, everything is in place. So run the game and enjoy your simple tank moving around, shooting at you.

Summary

In this chapter, we applied some of the AI techniques that we learned previously to our simple tanks combat game. Then, of course, we'd be able to use some more techniques in a larger game scope. Still, in this short chapter, we reused the simple FSM framework that we built in *Chapter 2*, *Finite State Machines*, as well as Unity's built-in navigation meshes capabilities.

This example project is a perfect starting point for exploring the AI techniques introduced in this book. You can implement many more improvements to the AI of this demo, and I encourage you to play with it a bit more. There are several pieces of low-hanging fruit, so here are my suggestions:

As a first exercise, you can increase the number of states, for instance, by adding a *Chasing* state in which the tank will actively look for the player. This structure is like the *Attack* state, but with a bigger radius. Then, as a more significant step, try to replace the FSM with a Behavior tree. The Behavior tree that we implemented in the Behavior tree demo is incredibly apt for this scenario. Finally, you need to change the script to call the correct function for the tank game, but it is an excellent exercise.

We hope that you learned something new in areas related to AI in games and Unity3D. We just scratched the surface of gameplay AI programming, but if you have reached the end of this book, you are suited for any challenge you may encounter in the future. Good luck, and have fun!

Index

`Packt.com`

Subscribe to our online digital library for full access to over 7,000 books and videos, as well as industry leading tools to help you plan your personal development and advance your career. For more information, please visit our website.

Why subscribe?

- Spend less time learning and more time coding with practical eBooks and Videos from over 4,000 industry professionals

- Improve your learning with Skill Plans built especially for you

- Get a free eBook or video every month

- Fully searchable for easy access to vital information

- Copy and paste, print, and bookmark content

Did you know that Packt offers eBook versions of every book published, with PDF and ePub files available? You can upgrade to the eBook version at `packt.com` and as a print book customer, you are entitled to a discount on the eBook copy. Get in touch with us at `customercare@packtpub.com` for more details.

At `www.packt.com`, you can also read a collection of free technical articles, sign up for a range of free newsletters, and receive exclusive discounts and offers on Packt books and eBooks.

Other Books You May Enjoy

If you enjoyed this book, you may be interested in these other books by Packt:

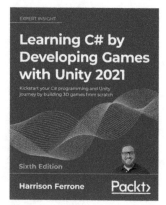

Learning C# by Developing Games with Unity 2021 – Sixth Edition

Scottie Crump

ISBN: 978-1-80181-394-5

- Follow simple steps and examples to create and implement C# scripts in Unity
- Develop a 3D mindset to build games that come to life
- Create basic game mechanics such as player controllers and shooting projectiles using C#
- Divide your code into pluggable building blocks using interfaces, abstract classes, and class extensions
- Become familiar with stacks, queues, exceptions, error handling, and other core C# concepts
- Learn how to handle text, XML, and JSON data to save and load your game data
- Explore the basics of AI for games and implement them to control enemy behavior

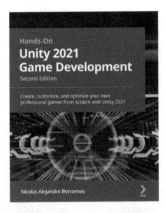

Hands-On Unity 2021 Game Development – Second Edition

Nicolas Alejandro Borromeo

ISBN: 978-1-80107-148-2

- Explore both C# and Visual Scripting tools to customize various aspects of a game, such as physics, gameplay, and the UI
- Program rich shaders and effects using Unity's new Shader Graph and Universal Render Pipeline
- Implement postprocessing to improve graphics quality with full-screen effects
- Create rich particle systems for your Unity games from scratch using VFX Graph and Shuriken
- Add animations to your game using the Animator, Cinemachine, and Timeline
- Use the brand new UI Toolkit package to create user interfaces
- Implement game AI to control character behavior

Packt is searching for authors like you

If you're interested in becoming an author for Packt, please visit authors. packtpub.com and apply today. We have worked with thousands of developers and tech professionals, just like you, to help them share their insight with the global tech community. You can make a general application, apply for a specific hot topic that we are recruiting an author for, or submit your own idea.

Share Your Thoughts

Now you've finished *Unity Artificial Intelligence Programming – Fifth Edition*, we'd love to hear your thoughts! Scan the QR code below to go straight to the Amazon review page for this book and share your feedback or leave a review on the site that you purchased it from.

https://www.amazon.in/review/1803238534

Your review is important to us and the tech community and will help us make sure we're delivering excellent quality content.

CPSIA information can be obtained
at www.ICGtesting.com
Printed in the USA
BVHW061938140922
647072BV00011B/182

9 781803 238531